Second Chance

Second Chance

A Life after Death

Marvin Barrett

 PARABOLA BOOKS

NEW YORK

Portions of this book have appeared in a slightly different form in
PARABOLA Magazine and in *The Best Spiritual Writing 1998*, edited by
Philip Zaleski (San Francisco: HarperSanFrancisco, 1998).

Published by the Society for the Study of Myth and Tradition
656 Broadway, New York, NY 10012

06 05 04 03 02 01 00 99
10 9 8 7 6 5 4 3 2 1

Library of Congress Cataloging-in-Publication Data

Barrett, Marvin.
    Second chance : a life after death / Marvin Barrett;
foreword by Rev. James Parks Morton.
        p.   cm.
    Sequel to: Spare days.
    ISBN 0-930407-42-3 (alk. paper).
    1. Barrett, Marvin. 2. Authors, American — 20th century — Biography.
3. Journalists — United States — Biography. 4. Near-death experiences.
    I. Title.
    PS3552.A7347 Z4628 1999
    818'.5403—dc21   98-44020
    [B]   CIP

The author and publisher gratefully acknowledge permission to reprint
the following material:

Excerpt from "An Ancient to Ancients" by Thomas Hardy. Reprinted
with the permission of Simon & Schuster from *The Complete Poems of
Thomas Hardy*, edited by James Gibson. Copyright © 1976 by
Macmillan London Ltd.

Lyrics to "Rockin' Chair" by Hoagy Carmichael. Copyright © 1930
by Peer International Corporation. Copyright renewed and international copyright secured. Used by permission.

Excerpt from *The Other Half* by Kenneth Clark. Reprinted by permission of John Murray Ltd.

Lyric excerpts from "I'm an Indian Too" by Irving Berlin. Copyright
© 1946 by Irving Berlin. Copyright renewed and international copyright secured. All rights reserved. Reprinted by permission.

Excerpt from *Number Our Days* by Barbara Myerhoff. Copyright ©
1978 by Barbara Myerhoff. Used by permission of Dutton, a division
of Penguin Putnam Inc.

Frontispiece: Detail from *Ascension to the Empireum* by Hieronymus Bosch.
Palazzo Ducale, Venice. Reprinted by permission of Art Resource, N.Y.

This book is dedicated to Mary Ellin,

my wife of forty-six years, and to my brother Dirk

in celebration of his eightieth birthday.

———

Foreword

"THE OLD ARE LIKE INDIANS—naturally noble, they have been degraded and put down. It is my concern to reinstate them to their former dignity." To accomplish this massive task Marvin Barrett begins with the proud acknowledgment of his own "old age." This is the necessary first step each of us must take: accepting the "label," "calling in" our "age credit." For without this recognition, there can be no vision, no second chance, and our culture of old folks' reservations in nursing homes won't change.

Vision and honesty, humor and love, are the touchstones of this book. Honest vision: to admit that life is not a series of detours with no main road, but to acknowledge that "you are and always have been on the highway and now the destination is clear and unavoidable." Barrett agrees with Salvador Dali that every old person is a hero because "heroism is quintessentially the conscious facing of death and holding firm."

And humor and love: the perception that "nothing about life can be dismissed as insignificant—a party, a facelift". . . "which means milking each encounter, each event for its ultimate meaning . . . and boredom disappears." Also with age "the need for comparison with others fades—who is smartest, prettiest, strongest . . . we recognize we are unique —no one is quite like . . . and at the same time . . . there is the growing experience of communion and sympathy with more and more of our fellow creatures."

Barrett agrees with Father Faber: "The surest method of arriving at a knowledge of God's eternal purpose about us is to be found in the right use of the present moment. God's will . . . comes to us . . . generally in small fragments. It is our business to piece it together." Barrett concludes "Trying to do good here and there is not such a cop out. . . ."

St. John of the Cross states, "When the evening of this life comes you will be judged on love." Barrett adds, "I see it as one's ability to love right now at the end of life . . . either as a fever of love . . . of a lifetime's regimen" or as "a sudden infection in which the prodigal son—doddering and gray-haired—shivering and hot with the emotion that has possessed him returns."

Old age is both the final leveler and everyone's second chance.

THE VERY REVEREND JAMES PARKS MORTON
Dean Emeritus, Cathedral of
St. John the Divine and President,
The Interfaith Center of New York

And now in age I bud againe

After so many deaths I live and write

I once more smell the dew and raine

And relish versing; O my onely light

It cannot bee

That I am hee

On whom thy tempest fell all night.

—George Herbert, "The Flowre"

Though leaves are many, the root is one;

Through all the lying days of my youth

I swayed my leaves and flowers in the sun;

Now I may wither into the truth.

—W. B. Yeats, "The Coming of Wisdom in Time"

A Life after Death

ON THE AFTERNOON of March 4, 1984, in the cardiac care unit of St. Luke's Hospital in upper Manhattan two months short of my sixty-fourth birthday, I died.

I didn't at the time know that that's what I was doing. However, a few days later my cardiologist, a no-nonsense fellow, with a half dozen young residents as witness, pointed to me in my hospital room and said, "On Sunday, that man was dead. *Dead.*" He repeated it to make sure we got the message. I had been brought back by the wonders of modern medicine, a sharp blow to the chest, a couple of electric paddles applied to my pectorals.

In the journal I was keeping at the time, I described the experience: "A green slope—not slippery, not furry—like sealskin—irregular but not bumpy, slipping but not grabbing to hold on. No panic—nothing disagreeable—the green very bright, like new grass. Not shale, no precipice. No one on the bank above cheering me on. Me alone; I am doing as I should. Letting go. Relaxed . . . Lots of light but not blinding . . . Then all of a sudden the delicious ride is over, the friendly green blinks out. The rattling and shaking, the dull roar, the low murmuring voices are back. I have returned."

If there was no tunnel with a light at the end, there was that seductive slope, smoother than those Olympic lugers plunge down, a free slide into the friendly unknown with light all round. If there was no life review—the instant replay of sixty-three years, fast backward—I had had, as a cancer patient in the previous seven months, plenty of time to summon up my past in intimate, sometimes acutely uncomfortable, detail.

That I was out of the body—that body lying on its hospital bed, the oscillating line of the screen above it flat—of that there was no question. But I hadn't, like some, floated up to the ceiling to oversee my own resuscitation, nor gone through walls to eavesdrop on frightened relatives assembled in the corridor outside. There was only one frightened relative out there—my wife, Mary Ellin, who had delivered me via patrol car to the hospital emergency bay an hour before. There had been no time to notify any of our four children, or concerned in-laws and friends, who were under the impression that finally Marvin was in the clear—the offending stomach, seat of a lymphoma, successfully removed; the course of radiation concluded. They had forgotten about my heart. We had all forgotten about my heart in our fascination with my stomach. And now, as it turned out, the slighted organ had done me in.

Done in, but still in those absent seconds my perceptions were unquestionably sharpened; and all pain, mental, physical, spiritual, was a thing of the past. An indescribable peace that required no explanation or understanding possessed me.

And there was the light. The gentle intensity of that ambient light, and the green of the slope—the combination one sometimes finds on a clear morning where fertile fields grow close to the sea, in the Low Countries that my ancestors came from, on the South Fork of Long Island where we spend half of each year—it was the light, and the peace accompanying it, that convinced me later, when I looked back, that I was indeed, for a brief interval, dead. Or if not completely dead, no longer conventionally alive; I was in another place, in another kind of time.

Nor had I quite made it back. Death, I told myself, when I was strong enough for such considerations, had deposited me on another shore, not the far shore from which there is no return, but the reef where old age begins. And the experience of death had made old age seem not a threat or a loss but a reprieve and a challenge.

We all have the privilege of naming the date of our old age and of anticipating our mood at its advent. A wise woman in my wife's family declared with an irony appropriate to an accomplished novelist, "Old age is ten years older than you are now," thus successfully avoiding the issue. But I was now saying my old age began ten, or at least six years, before my vigorous contemporaries would admit to that label. And I was welcoming it.

I had reasons other than "near death"—that reassuring dress rehearsal—for my provocative attitude. From earliest childhood I had always liked old people—sought them out, enjoyed their company, and that affection did not decline when I became a man. I didn't dread old age; if anything I had a hankering for it. I had a suspicion that it was not nearly so grim as many of my fellow Americans seemed to feel that it is, a suspicion that, appearances to the contrary, old age had no more drawbacks than any other stage in life—and maybe even a few advantages.

> *And when the strife is fierce, the warfare long*
> *Steals on the ear the distant triumph song,*
> *And hearts are brave again, and arms are strong.*
> *Alleluia, alleluia!*

That hymn, number 126 in the 1940 Episcopal hymnal, brings me to the business of faith, a faith instilled in me early on that life after all, on top of everything, against all odds, had meaning. This faith told me that with patience and love meaning could be discovered in each of life's successive stages, the open expanses of old age offering the last, most promising opportunity for revelation.

What follows are excerpts from my journals of the next seven years during which I contemplated death, old age, and life. It will be quite quickly clear that I write from the vantage point of a practicing Christian, but one who stands in awe of all the great faiths. My hope is that even those people who claim to be faithless, a category which includes most of my associates, who sooner or later will be traveling the same road, will find in these pages something to give them pause, and perhaps, heart.

My account begins in the fall of 1984 when after closing our farmhouse in Water Mill, Long Island and our Manhattan apartment, we set out for a part of the country which I hadn't visited in more than four decades. There as "an old man" I could put the distant past—with me a young naval officer on his way to war—alongside the immediate present and perhaps discover a new dimension in the juxtaposition.

1984

1984——

CRATER LAKE, OREGON. Six A.M. The cabin we booked yesterday, the last visitors before the snows set in, is cold and dark. I have dressed quickly and am pulling on my shoes when Mary Ellin stirs, groans, asks what time it is, says, "Oh, for God's sake Marvin, come back to bed. You're supposed to be taking it easy," and hides her head under the pillow.

Outside a crescent moon shines through high, thin clouds. There is one bright star in a clear patch of western sky: a yellow V in the east. The lake, bottomless blue, is silvered now—the sky slowly lightening—the rim of the ancient water-filled mountain black. On my side of the lake are tall pines; on the far shore, a low silhouette of hills. In the parking lot is one car. A jogger goes by calling out "good morning," his breath visible. A light comes on in the big shed that houses the store and cafeteria.

The yellow in the eastern sky widens; yellow turns to orange, orange to pink. A high cloud stretches above the hills with a belly of light under the furry black. One star is gone. Another. The morning star in the east still shines through the frail clouds. The moon is a crescent in a blurred circle just large enough to contain it.

I have always been addicted to sunrises but this one seems to carry a particular message and question. Why have

I survived to see a sunrise over Crater Lake? What am I, the barely recovered dead man, doing standing, inadequately clothed, in a frigid parking lot, admiring the view?

But then, shouldn't anyone who lives past sixty ask himself, ask herself, "Why have I survived to do anything? What am I doing here?" These are questions that should have been asked long ago. But now they are urgent. Why am I still here? How have I, who was dead last winter, arrived on the edge of this eerily beautiful, forbidding lake to watch the sunrise?

There can be no question that survival, on the shores of Crater Lake or anywhere, is the central miracle of life—the validating miracle—that we survive into the fertile egg, survive birth, infancy, childhood, adolescence—one threshold after another hesitantly, triumphantly crossed. Why shouldn't old age be the greatest triumph of all?

The sun is now up, white in the eastern sky. Buried in the dark western clouds, there is a smudged rainbow, a wavering circle of many colors, small, hovering, not arching, as though it had seeped through, and with no end in either direction. The lake is dark and deep and perfectly round.

Across the parking lot, Mary Ellin walks toward me looking cross. "It's been an hour. What are you doing? Where is your scarf? Why are you . . . ?" And then looking at the dark circle of the lake, the luminous sky above, she is silent.

The Abbot Bessarion, dying, said, "The monk should be all eyes, like the Cherubim and Seraphim." So, I say, should be the old, the about-to-be old.

—⚅—

TWO DAYS WITH THE REDWOODS, driving through them, walking in them. These trees have something to say about old age—the beauty and awesomeness of survival—independent of their enormous size, their silence, and their sheer extension in time. Still, you don't have the feeling of awe, as you do with old buildings, at what these stones have witnessed, or as you might have with rocks and fossils, that they were there millions of years ago when horrendous, amazing, unsurvivable things were going on. The redwoods have another kind of presence, a sort of being apart from memory and beyond the power to evoke past history. The possibility that one of these trees was alive here on this spot when on the opposite side of the earth Jesus was preaching or Nero fiddling seems irrelevant. They are the important thing, standing there, growing there. So is an aged human. But age is a credit that must be recognized and called in. One says, "I am old." I am old—and that is my identification, my label. Without acknowledgment there is no credit, no vision.

—ɯ—

SEATTLE. This is my first time back to this city since the spring of 1942 when, as an ensign in the Navy, I awaited assignment to the Aleutians—Adak, Dutch Harbor, or worse. I was fresh from a two-month stint of small-craft training in San Francisco Bay that didn't take, and a detour south for a conference with the English polymath Gerald Heard on the religious life, that did. I was a suddenly pious ensign, about to be a woefully unprepared executive officer on a mine sweep patrolling the stormy Bering Sea, a disaster waiting to happen.

And then, at the last minute, there was a miraculous reprieve, a temporary assignment to a desk job in Seattle, my papers mislaid. By the time they were found, eleven months later, I was up to six hours of prayer a day and had made two friends, Rose and Gustave Aschermann, who lived above Lincoln Park with an unobstructed view of

Puget Sound and, on fine days, the whole majestic straggle of the Olympics.

Disciples of Gerald Heard, the Aschermanns were small and spare, white-haired and wide-eyed. Rose was delicate as a feather, with a Louise Brooks bob and fluttering hands. Gustave was monolithic, Sumerian, not a wrinkle. "The simple life—" they said, welcoming me into their board-and-batten cabin, "We try to lead the simple life as best we can."

They read to each other, and to me, when I was around, their favorite books—"our blueprints for survival": Whitman, Edward Carpenter, Tolstoy, Ouspensky, Paul Buck, Vivekananda, Huxley, and Heard ("our beloved teacher"). They served me carrot loaf, spoonbread, tapioca, gluten-burgers, and shaggy mane mushrooms which Rose and I gathered in the park below. No smokes, no spirits, no meat. Starving me, boring me, soothing me. Youth encountered peaceful, uncomplaining old age and moved on, down the coast, across the Pacific, on his own trip. Now the youth is old himself—a resonant way to tell time.

The cabin, the steep garden, the spectacular view I had hoped to show Mary Ellin are gone, wiped out by a neighborhood of shingled condominiums.

"You must have been the navy's weirdest ensign," my wife tells me now, not for the first time. She too had been in Seattle before—in the late 1930s, a firm-gazed ten-year-old with black no-nonsense bangs, confidently boarding the yacht chartered by her father, Irving Berlin, the world-famous songwriter—a spoiled brat, ready for a month of having fun, fishing, exploring, loafing, playing games, an idle summer before the war without a glimmer of what would come next.

On the other side of town we visit Morgan O'Brien, Mary Ellin's cousin, who once with his raffish, well-heeled buddies was the terror of Southampton, Long Island. Now he is settled with his attractive Midwestern wife and two sturdy sons in a pleasant McKinley-style house on a street of such houses. Morgan in three generations has descended from indecent wealth to modest middle-class comfort.

We exchange family gossip. Aunt Kay's sapphires had gone to Uncle Bob's second wife, not to Cousin Katie as they should have. The mansion on the Truckee River where Aunt Kay reigned for many years as queen of Reno is now a museum.

Morgan, who in advancing years has not only given up drink and brawling but become a thoughtful Catholic, tells me that the very large solid silver crucifix bolted to the dining room wall had been a wedding gift from the notorious Boss Tweed to his parents.

"That is not possible," Mary Ellin corrects later back in our hotel room. "Boss Tweed was dead long before Aunt Kay and Uncle Ken were born, long before our Grandfather Mackay married our grandmother. You must have misunderstood. Or it is probably just another of Morgan's stories. Age may have dampened his carousing but not his tall tales."

—⚬—

HALFWAY UP MOUNT RAINIER, the holy mountain—we won't go higher, 5,000 feet is now my specified limit—Mary Ellin challenges me: "Don't be a fool. Sixty-four is not old."

"It is if I say it is. If I want it to be."

She shakes her head. She doesn't see the charm, the fascination, the advantage of being old. At home are her parents, her father ninety-seven, her mother eighty-one, not enjoying it a bit. *That* is old," she says as we drive back down. "Not you."

One of old age's reliefs, if not an absolute pleasure, should be the disappearance of the need always to be right, always

to stand up to someone younger's contention that we are
in error, to be able to hold, as the saying goes, our peace.

Still, without saying it, I am old.

If you will accept its credentials, age validates everything.
It is a real second chance—life itself being the first—another
opportunity without ambiguity—no shading, no tricks—
for those who haven't found their way and those who
have, alike.

Old age is the final leveler. It teaches the same lesson to
everyone, rich and poor, wise and foolish, learned and igno-
rant—to spoiled brat, weird ensign, and Southampton
playboy. We ask the same questions about the reason for
life—the use of life—the purpose of life—the meaning of
life—whatever you choose to call it. The mystery is like the
dark tarn of Crater Lake, or the bright saw of the Olympics
obliterated by a shingled condominium, or Mount Rainier
shrouded in mist, or the Oregon cliff off which a young man
in a hang glider sailed yesterday. He circled and then
dropped softly, trippingly in the sand at our feet where we
were having dinner in a small Pacific cove, the last flight,
the last fall before dark.

If one believes that old age offers something uniquely
worthwhile, better, or at least as good in its way as anything the earlier part of life offered—and I believe it does
—then relinquishing the prime-of-life prizes—their reality
(or more likely, their illusion), their hope, their possibility
—should be a natural gesture. And do we really have a
choice? Even if we are among those who have attained or
been given power, fame, beauty, talent, sexual satisfaction,
wealth (squandered or invested or hoarded), we will in the
face of old age eventually have to give them up, although
perhaps at the next-to-the-last minute.

But these are the very attachments that Christ, the
Buddha, all the sentimental nineteenth-century divines,

any spiritual director worth his or her salt, have said must go, or at least be ignored or looked beyond, if we are finally to understand. Instead for us the process of growing old too often induces panic—a spastic clutching at those very things that if we cling to them will surely sink us, and which already, earlier in life, have kept us from seeing, doing, being.

Freedom is, or should be, the synonym for old age—a free hand, a free view, the possibility of disinterested and significant thought and action—soaring and gently dropping, a free fall before night.

"He who lives with a sense for the presence knows that to get older does not mean to lose time but rather to gain time. And he also knows that in all his deeds, the chief task of man is to sanctify time. All it takes to sanctify time is God, a soul, and a moment. And the three are always here." Are we supposed to thank Rabbi Abraham Heschel, holy and hard-nosed, strictly twentieth century, for reminding us of this upsetting fact? But isn't to be upset the whole point?

—⟋⟋⟋—

ON THE COAST DRIVE. We have been warned, by sign after sign as we approach, of "an experience not to be missed," the cave of the sea lions. A ticket booth, an elevator descending through live rock, and there the sea lions are in their towering grotto in the flickering water-refracted light, yelping, moaning, halumphing from rock to rock with their formidable hips glistening, more hips than an hippopotamus. It is, I suddenly recognize it, the first act of *Tannhauser*, and we are the audience, who stand transfixed, ignoring the horrid smell, and seeing the reflection in the wobbling, shimmering water of the western sea—Venusburg minus the goddess.

But there is someone in charge, on a high rock surveying all the noise and confusion—an old bull, greying and serene.

A morning is spent wandering through a dark, twisted forest of petrified trees, broken trunks and branches embedded in, and struggling out of, a grey frozen sludge of lava, a catastrophe six thousand years old.

SAN FRANCISCO

THE SECOND most beautiful city on earth. Elizabeth, our oldest child, has chosen well: a talented composer husband, and a home at the top of a hill, the third floor of a grey wooden survivor of the great earthquake and fire of 1906, high-ceilinged and spacious.

We visit her at the job she loves; she is librarian in a small girls' school, recommending and reading her favorite books to children like those we hope some day she will have. Slender, with long, shiny hair, her mother's elegant features and widely spaced hazel eyes, she bends over the youngsters gathered in a circle around her, the floor striped with the slanting California light.

It has been a morning of churches. Glide Memorial at nine with the flower children in calico and jeans praying for the old; Grace Cathedral at eleven with the old folks in flannels and Liberty prints and the well-dressed middle-aged out in numbers praying for everyone, including themselves.

When I was a teenager it seemed that a disproportionate number of people in church were old. My grandparents and those of their generation were the church regulars. My parents and their contemporaries, except for the Catholics and the Jews and a few maiden ladies, had mostly foresworn the comforts and inconveniences of faith in favor of the more obvious satisfactions of maturity. There is time enough, with your wits, your senses dulled, your courage failed, your family scattered, for you to turn back, to become that old gentleman sitting silent in a forward pew, that old lady telling her beads in front of the Virgin and the banks of guttering candles.

Now I acknowledge openly that such devotion is desirable at any age, in any condition, and it seems that, at least this morning, the world agrees.

Living with old age is rather like living in San Francisco. You know at some moment, any moment, the terminal cataclysm may come, and you and this magnificent place surrounding you will go up in flames, down in a torrent of bricks, be engulfed in a wall of water. But when you are young, as Elizabeth and her husband Sasha are, you are right to ignore the threat that seems more than balanced by the beauty, the good living. You can't take each step or breath or bite as though it may be your last and in the next instant the amazing stage-set will be struck and there will be no place to put your foot, lay your head, or set your teeth.

Still the precariousness is a fact, and not only for you, but for everyone. Remembering it and forgetting it are pretty much the same. And there in your head is Jeannette MacDonald singing her heart out as the chandeliers begin to sway.

— ᴍ —

ON THE FLIGHT HOME my reading is *And There Was Light*, the remarkable autobiography of a blind French civil servant, Jacques Lusseyran. As a teenager he was a leader of the Resistance who ended up in Buchenwald. His observations, sharpened by his blindness and peril:

Last of all there were the old men, the old Russians and all the rest, the French, the Poles, the Germans. From them too I always learned something. Because, you see, the bad old men, all those who hadn't found out how to grow old, had died. At Buchenwald many died between fifty and sixty-five. That was the age for the great slaughter, and almost all the survivors were good men.

As for them, they were no longer there. They were looking at the world, with Buchenwald in the middle of it, from further away. They absorbed Buchenwald as part of the great outpouring of the universe, but already they seemed to belong to a better world. I found nothing but gladness in the men over seventy.

That is what you had to do to live in the camp: be engaged, not live for yourself alone. The self-centered life has no place in the world of the deported. You must go beyond it, lay hold on something outside yourself. Never mind how: by prayer if you know how to pray; through another man's warmth which communicates with yours, or through yours which you pass on to him; or simply by no longer being greedy. Those happy old men were like the hoboes. They asked nothing more for themselves, and that put everything within their reach.

WATER MILL, LONG ISLAND

THE DOG HAS BEEN HERE two and a half days now. One of the things I thought of first when I was told I had cancer, that some sort of definite term might have been put to my life, was that I'd get myself a dog to help mark the time.

And now, the dog's arrival has been made by me into an occasion for panic—or worse than that—anxiety and guilt.

Two years ago the Columbia University/DuPont Awards would have been what kept me awake. The TV show celebrated "the Pulitzers of Broadcast Journalism" which were my responsibility. Then my anxiety was concerned with the mistakes I could have made with the whole world watching, the unpredictable news anchors who were my star performers given free rein, their egos rampant.

Now anxiety has become the dog and guilt the cat. The cat, my first acquisition to celebrate my retirement, was named Pippo for San Filippo Neri and/or Phillips Brooks—both big, peaceful, holy men. Pippo is a big, placid cat but now he seems to be brooding, is off his food; it is my fault for bringing this larger, darker, doggy presence into his territory. And the dog: What is that thin patch on her back? Is she really happy in her new home? Healthy? Am I, in my frail condition, up to her care and exercise? (Mary Ellin is not a dog person.) Wasn't it irresponsible of me to even think, after all these dogless years, of acquiring a dog, and a big one at that?

Anxiety is the crab that fixes itself on something, anything, no matter how large or small, how fresh or spoiled. The crab I had to shake free from the seaman's knitted cap I found on the beach this afternoon, intact, washed across the sea—the sailor now inhabited by crabs, of coral made. The crab—cancer—a feeder on the young and old alike.

The dog, named Molly, is one of the first Portuguese Water Dogs to be bred on this side of the ocean, an "important" animal, according to the Animal Rescue Fund, although she is barely three years old and up for adoption free of charge. Her actual name is *Condesa do Mar*, "Countess of the Sea."

The vet tells me she is strong and well and the thin patch

is a seasonal allergy that will disappear. Pippo the cat has
come out of his funk. And now it is Mary Ellin I have to
worry about: How will she put up with the dog's sleeping
on the sofa? And where now will the cat sleep? And so it
goes—until I acknowledge my age and my opportunity, my
duty as an old man to be guiltless and anxiety free. Fussing,
the last resort of the under-occupied, must go as well.

Lohan Hoshang of Shoshu, a Chinese Buddhist, recounts
how a Master he met on his wanderings resolved all his
anxieties by a blow to his chest.

> This all of a sudden exploded my lump of doubt
>   completely in pieces.
> Raising my head, I perceived for the first time that
>   the sun was circular.
> Since then I have been the happiest man in the
>   world, with no fears, no worries.
> Day in, day out, I pass my time in a most lively way.
> Only I notice my inside filled with a sense of fullness
>   and satisfaction.
> I do not go out any longer, hither and thither, with
>   my begging bowl.

Such a blow was essentially how I was brought back from
death at St. Luke's Hospital. It was no C'han Master who
struck me on the chest, but a young Jewish intern. The
paddles followed. As for fears and worries, that remains to
be seen.

It is a brilliant, cool day. Among the roseate finches at
the feeder there was, for a moment, a gold one. Although
Pippo is attentive, waiting upon chance to deliver him an
inattentive bird, Molly is indifferent to both the rabbits in

the backyard and the chipmunks who loiter beneath the feeder to catch falling seed. Nor, despite her breed, does she fancy the water when I take her to the beach. High-spirited and carefree, off her leash she bounds into the dunes. She has none of that nervous alertness that possesses hunters of any sex or species, no fears, no worries. She barks when Mary Ellin and I stand talking by the kitchen counter. To stop us? To join us? To get us to sit down and take it easy?

IOWA

IN RESPONSE to a cousin's invitation to a family reunion, we are traveling again. "I don't know that I saved your life to go for a long weekend in Des Moines," my wife tells me.

"You saved my life?"

Mary Ellin explains it wasn't anything so simple as commandeering a patrol car and getting me to the hospital in the nick of time. "It was telling whoever or whatever was up there (she points to the plane's ceiling) not to let you die."

"Well, " I reply. "You know what that means. To save someone's life makes you responsible for them from then on, however long that may be, however ungrateful and disagreeable they are or may become."

"I know."

"Even for a long weekend in Des Moines."

"Is that a threat?"

It has been nearly forty years since I lived in Des Moines— this place which every baggy-pants comic, every late-night TV host considers fair game. Fourteen years since I paid my last visit (with my wife, our four children, three teenagers, and a fresh ten-year-old, plus a daughter's boyfriend along for the hilarious ride). But as far as my memories and my dreams are concerned, Des Moines is no joke.

This city which blurs in every direction into open fields remains my home. It is where I grew up, where my mother and father and his mother were born and raised—the capital of a state where two of my great grandfathers, a Scotch blacksmith and a Dutch cabinet maker, were pioneers.

Now the cousins on the Dutch, the Kruidenier side of the family, a grey-haired lot—some better dressed, some friendlier than others—are converging for a reunion in Des Moines and Pella, the small farming community where most of us share our roots. We are here to honor the relative we have in common, Daniel the cabinet maker.

On my last visit here I was still concerned about the effect my Eastern wife and children might have on the members of the family who had stayed on, and their effect on us. Now, thanks to my new disposition, I have no such concern. Whatever our current abode, our destination is the same.

The Des Moines of my dreams and memory is a leafy place with spreading elms, low-pitched roofs, and quiet front yards. But the giant trees which once made an arching corridor of the town's main thoroughfare, and canopied its parks and lawns, are long since gone, destroyed by elm disease. And the city's center looks as though it had been ground under some giant heel of glass and steel, and the heel had become the city. The fusty downtown of fifty years ago now is a clump of glassy skyscrapers connected by elevated walks. A plaza with a giant Oldenburg umbrella has replaced the rundown Coliseum where Nijinsky, Chaliapin, Paderewski, Kreisler, and Madame Schuman-Heink had once performed and which, by my time, was accommodating the dog show, the auto show, and Aimee Semple Macpherson.

As a freshman on a shaky scholarship (three B's and a C at November hours) returning from Harvard, I remember thinking that Des Moines, which seemed so large and authentic when I left, was no city at all but a dirty smudge pinned to the prairie by the white-topped Equitable Life Insurance Building, the tallest in the state. There on the eighteenth floor my Aunt Ada Barrett (the other side of the family) sat at her desk passing judgment on claims mailed in by the heirs of recently dead farmers. What a thrill it was to take the elevator to the top floor, stare down from her window at the gold-domed capitol, the fair grounds beyond, knowing that in the corner office sat Aunt Ada's boss, the richest, most important man in all of Iowa.

Now the Equitable is only the fourth tallest building in town, a greying spindle surrounded by shining, towering boxes.

At the top of one of those shining boxes in a new penthouse club, we have dinner the night of our arrival with Cousin David, once a stocky little boy with a scowl, now publisher of the *Des Moines Register*—a leading citizen, smart, affable, with an edge—and a highly intelligent, good-looking lawyer wife. During most of the dinner he and Mary Ellin are deep in conversation. "What were you talking about?" I ask her afterwards. "*Your* subject," she answers. "Old age." They had been discussing his mother, my Aunt Florence, at the far end of her eighties, and Mary Ellin's father, halfway through his nineties.

The question was, Who is worse off—the frail, querulous but clear-in-the-head old man, waiting it out in his top floor hideaway in New York City overlooking the East River, or the old lady, healthy, cheerful and gaga in a luxury condominium in La Jolla—one minutely aware of his condition and deploring it, the other happy in her oblivion? It was, of course, no contest. The clear head and misery won out.

. . .

If Des Moines, elmless and glassed over, is an affront, Pella,
fifty miles to the south and east, where the chartered bus
full of aging Kruideniers takes us, is quite another thing.
The Dutch built to last. The trees and tulip beds remain.
Three of Grandfather Dirk's houses stand, one house cut in
half to make two. A fourth, burnt to the ground, is back in
replica. The town square where Dirk and his brother
Lenhardt had their general store, where cousin Herman Van
Zante's hardware emporium was just off the corner (on
each visit he gave my brother and me new wooden shoes),
is as I remember it. There is Jaarsma's bakery where
each Christmas my mother ordered our initials in almond-
filled pastry. There is the butcher where we bought Dutch
baloney and *kumine kaas*, the cheese filled with tiny fragrant
seeds which you could buy nowhere else. Nothing seems
expanded, nothing decayed. Even the people, farmers and
solid Dutch burghers, look the same, although I am already
three generations past my first memory. And above us is a
red and brown mackerel sky, a prairie sunset I had almost
forgotten.

We are in for a long evening of food and family chat-
ter, and a program to celebrate Great-grandfather Daniel,
the cabinet maker, at Central College in the austere modern
building that is being given in his name by Cousin David.

The gentleman on stage, no relative of ours but a histo-
rian, knows more about our ancestors than we do: Great-
grandfather Daniel arrived in 1855 from Rotterdam by
packet, six weeks to cross the North Atlantic, another three
weeks by train, and finally a wagon with a canvas cover to
protect his wife and eight children, his household, and his
tools—ready to set up shop on the Iowa prairie.

The Dutch, unlike the Irish, the Mediterraneans, and the

Eastern Europeans, arrived, our friend on stage tells us, "complete." No rags to riches stories as in Mary Ellin's family, no tenement or mining-camp squalor to rise above—no waiting for, or going back to fetch abandoned wives and children. The Dutch came with expectations defined. And Pella, where the Rotterdam Kruideniers settled, drew a classier crowd than Holland, Michigan, the Midwest's premier Dutch settlement where my mother's mother, Wilhelmina Plugger, the daughter of a Great Lakes shipowner, was born and raised.

This great-grandfather, who lived to eighty-eight, seems beyond the grasp of my imagination—although when all of us, one by one, his male descendants, have our pictures taken standing by his portrait, I am told I am the most like.

The next generation is within reach. Daniel's youngest son, Dirk, my grandfather, though he died four years before I was born, is accessible to my mind. I can chart the trajectory of his life—his solid success as a small town merchant, the houses he built in Pella which he and his family eventually outgrew, the farms and business he bought to leave to his three sons. It was he who moved the family from Pella to Des Moines, the state capital.

I too can participate in the simple domestic horror of his death during a family dinner, as recalled by my cousin Ed, the oldest grandchild, then aged four, who was there to witness it. Who else was present besides little Ed? My three uncles, Leonard, David and Edward? Aunt May, Edward's pretty, unhappy wife? My own mother, the youngest (she never mentioned it), her older sisters, Elizabeth and Helene? My grandmother, certainly. She would have supervised the preparation and serving of the meal. She was suddenly brutally bereaved by a man too young to die—a man my age. Ed, a precise, elegantly dressed bachelor, is now himself past seventy.

—ɯ—

THE NEXT DAY in Des Moines, a grey day, very grey, with fat heavy clouds, fatter and greyer than we get in the East. Cousins Catherine and Angelica, daughter and grand-daughter of Uncle Leonard, drive us to the family cemetery.

At the bottom of Grand Avenue, a funeral cortege cuts in ahead of us—a hearse, two big black autos filled with family, followed by a leisurely procession of perhaps fifty nondescript cars with their lights on. (On the Long Island Expressway the processions, limousines only, go as fast as the rest of us.)

We wait, then follow the cars up the avenue and turn off at 42nd Street to catch a glimpse of my Kruidenier uncles' houses, south of Grand, once huge, now modestly large, comfortable, tenanted by strangers.

Back on Grand Avenue I point out Grandfather Barrett's house where, at the bottom of the walk, on Sunday after-noons we would wait in our Chevrolet while my father's father went through the rooms for the third time, checking every door—front, back and cellar—the refrigerator, the fur-nace, puttering, pottering, putting off to the last moment his departure. In this dwelling his wife of forty years had recently died and his son Bill, his daughter-in-law, and granddaughter occupied cramped quarters on the third floor.

Uncle Bill—I remember him vividly—was restless like myself, eager to explore another world beyond the one he was born into. In my memory there is Bill with his patent leather hair, in his band leader's tux, the accordion on his flat belly all buttons and bellows, mother-of-pearl and daz-zling white teeth—accordion and Uncle Bill both. *Bill Barrett's Cardinals* said his letterhead with a bright red bird in the upper left-hand corner. His band covered Iowa, ven-turing as far south and west as Kansas City (Jimmy

Lunceford, Count Basie, and Julia Lee), and north to the suburbs of Chicago (Bix and Louie)—he knew them all. Reefer madness—no, not quite that, a drag or two between sets. The accordion was regularly hocked. Grandpa Barrett just as regularly redeemed it; he wasn't as mean as he sometimes seemed, at least not where Bill was concerned. Bill ended up in Southern California, clerking in a neighborhood hardware store.

At the cemetery the funeral is there ahead of us, a crowd gathered by a tent set up on the slope across from the Kruidenier family plot, heads bowed, a man in black holding a book.

Strangely, the graveyard does not seem to have spread and grown like the town around it, no new stretches opened and covered with graves. Those graves already there have been stripped of their special plantings—no flowers, no bushes, just grass, healthy weedless grass, well kept. Grandmother and Grandfather Kruidenier, Helene, Ed, David—all are buried there at the foot of the big weatherstained granite obelisk. Mother and Uncle Leonard are in San Diego where most of the family ended up until they were shipped back in boxes to this final resting place; Aunt Elizabeth, the family rebel, the oldest and best-looking of a handsome brood, is I don't know where.

We go on north to the Barrett plot. Again a grandfather and a grandmother, William Edwin, Letta Galbraith, Aunt Ada, and my brother Eddie—Edwin Galbraith Barrett, 1925–1928. Dead before his elders, he is the only one of my generation, Kruidenier or Barrett, buried here.

The small white house with the pillared porch, 1408 Forestdale Drive, where I spent the first eighteen years of my life, plus two—and return to at least once a fortnight in my dreams. It is still there, apparently unchanged.

A young man in shirtsleeves opens the door; behind him

is a heavily pregnant young woman and deeper in the shadows of the living room a silent, ancient parent. They invite us in, since that is what we seem to want. Their taste isn't my mother's but the living room is recognizable, the same size and shape, the same windows and beamed ceiling, fireplace and mantel. I could furnish it from memory: the high-backed wicker chair with the hollow arms for magazines or darning that my mother kept repainting until it ended a defiant Chinese red; the gutted player piano in the far corner, on the music rack "The Song Is Ended," "Chloe," "The World is Waiting for the Sunrise," "The Indian Love Lyrics."

"Pale hands I loved beside the Shalimar; Where are you now?" Poppa sang in his formidable bass with his accompanist Cousin Nellie, a small spare woman with strong hands at the piano. "And now, perhaps Marvin will favor us with a selection." "The Scarf Dance"—my recital piece. We were a musical family.

Under the front windows was the daybed, Great-grandfather Daniel's master work—made of native walnut, spooled and finialed with a gracefully curved back and legs. They laid me on it the winter I fractured my skull in a sledding accident and watched me aghast as I left them. "Gone," said the family doctor, and then gave me the shot that brought me back—the first of my miraculous round trips.

It was the year my brother Eddie was born.

Upstairs in the attic where my brother Dirk and I slept (the baby had been given our downstairs bedroom) the dormer windows in winter were frozen fast and thick with frost, and in summer opened wide to invite a nonexistent breeze. The current owners have added air conditioning and a bathroom to accommodate Grandma. The house that was built to greet me on my arrival on the planet is scrubbed with a shine to it. It is obviously still cherished.

At the top of the hill we pass the curb where I stood and saw Eddie destroyed. One minute I was holding his hand, the next my hand was empty. The car—the sound of tires on macadam—the bonny boy reduced to a dull thud that I'll never forget.

On the plane home we ask ourselves about our long weekend. Whatever else, it certainly had not been boring. But had it raised ghosts or laid them to rest? "Do you wish you had never left?" is one of the questions Mary Ellin asks sometimes, hoping to catch me unawares.

"No," I say firmly, but not at once.

Mary Ellin pauses and then tells me about the rest of her conversation with Cousin David that first night. How my brother Eddie's death not only lowered my family into deep shadow, but cast a pall on David's own privileged childhood. How he and his sisters were told more than once what might happen to them if they didn't look both ways before crossing the street. They had been introduced to the reality of death, although in their neighborhood with its broad lawns and long driveways the threat of traffic, of death, seemed dim and distant. "Look both ways," a lesson for kids and for the aging grown-ups we had all become.

"You must live," our family osteopath had told me, a shaky young man on his first desperate return after four years of war and a disastrous year at a West Coast religious commune, "as if today were your last, and as if you would live forever." Dr. P., a tall statue of a woman with a magnificent head of Titian hair and strong arms, was the family love object and sibyl. "Marvin," she would say as she kneaded my back and cracked my vertebrae, "Just remember this: Tomorrow is the first day of the rest of your life."

Had my dying last March confirmed Dr. P.'s cross-stitch

platitudes or ripped them out? I look at Mary Ellin in the seat beside me, the current woman-in-charge, for a long time now—and refrain from asking.

NEW YORK AND WATER MILL

BACK HOME on Claremont Avenue, I was called to the phone to speak to my new hotshot editor. He was much displeased that I hadn't met the deadline for the book I had promised months before, an autobiography cantilevered from my youthful reminiscences of Ronald Reagan from the time when he had been a sports announcer on radio station WHO, Iowa's clear-channel station, heard as far away as Schenectady to the east, and Butte, Montana to the west. There, at WHO, my father, brother Dirk, and I—"Captain Bill, Jimmy and Teddy"—fed the young Dutch Reagan the largest audience of ten-year-olds in the Middle West. In addition to Reagan, who soon decamped for Hollywood, there were also to be recollections of Joan Crawford, Laurence Olivier, John Huston, Pat Weaver, Charles Van Doren, Elsa Maxwell—characters my work as a journalist had brought me into contact with—and also Hugh Hefner and Huntington Hartford, my colorful sometime bosses. This project, a lifetime of jerry-built celebrity anecdotes with flimsy morals attached, was one I no longer had any enthusiasm for. The present, I told myself, was what I was interested in, even though it frequently seemed simply an opportunity to revisit and reevaluate the past. Still it was me, an old man, doing the reevaluating.

This pipsqueak editor—I have already forgotten his name—expressed a cool displeasure at my tardiness, and a total indifference to the story of my illness, in the six hundred pages I was cutting to a manageable three hundred and offering him in the other book's place. I felt no answering resentment to his snub—no concern about what he might think or do if I didn't respond appropriately to his demands. The space where he should have been, above me glaring threateningly down, was empty. He wasn't getting through to me at all.

Such is the immunity and indulgence, I decided, of seniority. This intentionally disagreeable young man was another of God's creatures whether or not he appreciated and acted like it. He couldn't really do me lasting harm, nor I him. I should have told him just that if I had wanted to drive him up the wall. But I remained silent, more than content with the realization that in a lifetime of deadlines I had met my last, at least of the kind imposed by someone else. There was to be no more jumping in answer to another's snapping fingers. He was welcome to his advance, all $1,500 of it—the check would be in the mail tomorrow.

A surprised silence was followed by a grunt. "Give my best to my old buddy M. (his boss)," I said, and rang off happy.

—ɷ—

A DREAM LAST NIGHT in which I was bleak and hopeless, complaining that my writing had gained no acceptance and my acting (my acting?!) the same. But in the dream I was a young man with all my life ahead of me. And when I woke I was old and full of hope, hopeful about what I could and should and possibly still would do. In recent weeks bad dreams, good days has become the customary trade off. A fair exchange.

Meanwhile the evidence piles up day by day—at least on the good ones—"the deeper the mystery, the greater the wonder." I say it again, to myself, to whoever will listen. Our true survival depends on our belief that life has meaning—total meaning, from beginning to end, a meaning that includes not only all of our life—every minute, bad days, good days alike—but every other creature, good or bad, without exception. No thing—no one—can be dismissed or ignored. All is evidence and opportunity: a dream, a phone call. Any shadow, any doubt is simply a preparation for more light, more certainty.

—ᴧᴧ—

YESTERDAY we spent the evening with the Lerners, Max and Edna, in their apartment with its view down the East River, the New York skyline bright on the bank. Max was just back from California, preparing for his six-lecture series at the New School and then, after the holidays, ready to go back to the West Coast for the second semester at the University of California at Irvine. He continues to write three columns a week and works on his various book projects— at least four that I know of. Next month he will be presented at grand rounds at Mount Sinai Hospital by Doctors Holland and Hollander as the most glowing example of the success of their new cancer therapy. All this at eighty-two—and under this activity one senses an acceptance of his mortality on his own terms—his terms obviously being very vigorous ones.

Edna, the mother of his three sons, silver blonde and handsome, her magnificent profile slightly tilted, sat serene at her end of the table, commenting from time to time, correcting the conversation's thrust in her shaded drawl.

Somewhere in all the talk Max found occasion to quote Wordsworth: "Bliss was it in that dawn to be alive, But to be young was very heaven!"

Another dinner with the Lerners, this time at their farmhouse in Southampton. With dessert Max asked us to identify the people we most admired. Jeffrey Potter, another writer friend, spoke of a Sikh officer in Burma during World War II who taught him how to dispatch the mortally wounded soldiers who were moaning in the rice paddies revealing their location to the enemy. You lay next to them breathing more and more slowly, said Jeffrey, until, when you held your breath, they died. He didn't tell us how many soldiers he dispatched that way nor did he admit to feeling any particular tenderness for the men lying there, helpless and dying.

Then Jeffrey modulated into the story of how he had connived with his mother in her death at the age of ninety-four. He bullied the attendant physician into going along by uncovering an unfortunate lapse in the doctor's past.

Jeffrey took a stoutly secular approach in all of this although his grandfather and three great-uncles were bishops, one of whom had proclaimed from the pulpit to a cowed congregation, "We are the Potters, ye the clay." No wonder that when he finally got himself confirmed in his ancestors' church in his sixties he fainted under the anointing bishop's hand.

—ɯ—

THANKSGIVING. Three of our children are present: Irving, Mary Ellin, Katherine—all busy, in flux. Irving is preparing to move to the East Village to go after his art in earnest. Mary Ellin Jr. is contemplating a job in Washington, D.C. with *USA Today*. Katherine, back from Italy, is working at *Cosmopolitan*, making up her mind about the academic career she intends to pursue. Only Elizabeth, the eldest, is absent. Everyone has his or her own agenda and opinions, which are expressed without any reticence. All of them at least one time in the last two decades have been in grave peril, and all released—the Barrett luck. My family—one good reason I have survived.

There are a few skeptical comments on the large portrait recently arrived on our dining room wall, of Katherine
Duer Mackay Blake, my wife's grandmother, a bad luck lady
if there ever was one. Three generations distant, the famous
beauty gazes down with troubled eyes on the noisy, good-
looking Barretts, her great-grandchildren. Those eyes signal
her brains (a novel or two, the company of intellectuals),
her privilege (old New York married to great new riches
from the West), her notoriety (a scandalous divorce), her
misery (abandoned finally by the heartless interloper), and
her untimely death (the cancer that killed her was already
growing behind those phenomenal eyes). Her tragedy was
assigned and delivered long before old age could give its
release—gone to Woodlawn at fifty. For all its beauty and
panache there is a melancholy about the portrait: the dress
and the jewels opulent and out of date, the gesture of the
elegant hand.

Under her sad gaze I carve the turkey as usual—no interruption there, no volunteers. My children and my juniors,
which means everyone at the table, are considerate. Should
I falter they would be there to assist. Until then they are
content to look on, to witness this evidence that Dad, that
Marvin, is back to normal, though exiled from an office
and an assigned job. (In the front hall in boxes yet to be
unpacked is a lifetime's accumulation.)

I say a cautious grace. It is the first Thanksgiving after
death.

—◦◦◦—

A VISIT TO BERT DAGMAR, the charge given me by the
West Side Ministry to the Elderly four years ago, when
elderliness had a different meaning. A former vaudevillian,
night club M.C., and radio host, he sits in his bathrobe, dentures out, in his Upper West Side single room occupancy

hotel surrounded by memorabilia of the good old days at the Palace, in Atlantic City, on WNEW. On the wall are pictures of Kiki Roberts, Legs Diamond's delectable girlfriend, Bert's friend as well, and Helen Morgan whom he had comforted, he tells me, in her drunken despair backstage in an Atlantic City dive.

Bert is somewhere in the neighborhood of ninety, although being a professional entertainer and orphan his dates are dim. He was not only an entertainer but a bartender and floorwalker filling in the gaps between engagements, a lot of gaps since World War I.

Today he is grieving for his mother, lost at birth, and for his failing strength and faculties. "Why me?" he asks. "Oh, God, why me?" An odd question at his age, and useless at any age. I hardly feel worthy of instructing him in such matters when my own tuition is so recent and shaky.

Instead I give him two bottles of champagne—one for Christmas and the other for New Year's—and a box of chocolates for his caretaker, a large, comfortable woman who is, I fear, getting restless.

On the bus home, an old fellow with a pail and harness argues me into a seat which I offer to him since he had obviously come from washing windows—what I perceive as a strenuous, perhaps dangerous, job.

"Oh, no," he says. "Four hours a day maximum. I am my own boss. I work as long as I please. After the holidays I will go to South America. Cartagena. Then on to Venezuela for six weeks or so."

He tells me he is seventy-seven, a dozen years my senior, and there I sit with him looking down at me. An orphan, he says. Like Mr. Dagmar. But whereas Mr. D. had been sent West with a trainload of orphans by some well-meaning clergyman to be brutalized by his supposed benefactors and released into a hostile world as an unprepared teenager, this fellow was well treated. He was given a good education and a trade—printing. No wife, no family responsibilities—why is he telling me all this? He was a paratrooper in World War II, volunteering at thirty-four, got a couple of purple hearts.

I tell him that at seventy-seven, still washing windows and taking junkets to a perilous South America, he is some kind of freak. He shrugs and accepts the description as it is intended, a compliment.

Thoughts for Christmas morning: If you conceive of life as an adventure, the whole of life must be the adventure—not just the beginning and the middle—and like everything up till then, the end is open and uncertain. Otherwise, where is the adventure? Or, if you think of life as a gift, the whole of life must be the gift—not just what we think may be its blessings. Or, to truly learn is to realize that your life up until this moment has been one long lesson; the test comes later. Or this from the Sufis—"A sick man lay groaning in the presence of the Prophet and one of the Companions told him to stop and be patient, whereupon the Prophet said: 'Let him groan, for groaning is one of the names of God in which the sick man may find relief.'"

1985

1985—

NEW YEAR'S DAY. An item in the morning paper.

Philadelphia, Dec., 31, 1984 (UPI)

Massa, the oldest gorilla in captivity died of an apparent stroke late Sunday shortly after celebrating his fifty-fourth birthday with a special meal.

Zoo officials said today that in the wild, an African gorilla would probably live no more than twenty-five years.

"We are saddened by this loss of our most beloved resident," said William Donaldson, president of the Philadelphia Zoo. "We are grateful that he passed away peacefully."

An autopsy showed the immediate cause of death was a blockage of the arteries in the brain. It also found that Massa suffered from severe generalized hardening of the arteries . . .

Massa feasted Sunday afternoon on vanilla ice cream and fruits topped with whipped cream on a high-protein cake as about five hundred people watched.

"He wasn't fed an extra large dose of food," said Deborah Derrickson, a zoo spokesman. "We do not think the party contributed to his death." She said the party foods had been approved by the zoo's dietitian.

Massa's brain will go to Johns Hopkins University in Baltimore and Montefiore Hospital in New York, where neuropathologists will look for signs of Alzheimer's disease.

— ∿ —

CATCHING UP WITH PERSIS. Wandering through the Grant Wood exhibit at the Whitney Museum in New York City some months back—walls of Iowa scenes, Iowa faces, Iowa opinions translated into careful two dimensional packages— I was suddenly confronted with a photograph of my Aunt Florence on a sketching expedition in Stone City. She sat on a hillside filled with other young artists, drawing pads in their laps. Standing above her was a farmer in overalls, who might have wandered in from one of the master's own paintings. Below her, in a white tennis dress, a scarf twisted around her head, was Persis Robertson, her almost pretty face (the nose and chin were too strong for real prettiness) in deep concentration.

Persis, a classmate of my parents at West High in Des Moines, was the daughter of an important Iowa lawyer, who had been a vice presidential candidate on an unsuccessful ticket in the early 1900s. Her brother was a scientist, one of the men who perfected color photography; her husband a prosperous Iowa banker. For a year or two her older daughter, Madeline, red-haired and sharp-tongued, was my favorite partner at junior high school dances, twelve- and thirteen-year-olds dressed in inappropriately grown-up clothes doing the Carioca and a bowdlerized version of the Continental—"You (didn't) kiss while you're dancing."

After Madeline went away to boarding school, Persis took it upon herself to maintain the friendship, a simple matter of her lending me books and eliciting my reactions to them, force-feeding me the poems of Hopkins, Jeffers, Pound, Eliot, Hart Crane, and the novels of Virginia Woolf,

Proust, Joyce, Mann, James Branch Cabell. Actually there was little force involved. I would, she found, read anything and ask for more.

Albert, her banker husband, was puzzled by these conferences of Persis with a spotty adolescent in the big, book-lined house, south of Grand Avenue. Her aged father occasionally peered out from his corner study to see who was waiting for his daughter, and seeing me, quickly withdrew. The eager young man, the obliging older woman—a scene, strictly cerebral in this case, played out in who-knows-how-many parlors across the land.

Later, when I was home from Harvard, waiting for my navy orders, it was Persis who insisted (by then *she* was reading the books I recommended) that I get in touch with Gerald Heard, my current enthusiasm, a miracle man who knew everything there was to know about science and religion and saw no conflict between them.

I hadn't seen Persis since she paid us a visit on Long Island twenty years ago. The young woman on the museum wall was a reminder and a reproach.

Madeline, now a grey-haired grandmother many times over, and one of my few Des Moines friends to end up in Manhattan, gave me her mother's address, a retirement community in Bridgeport, Connecticut. "She is in splendid shape. She'd love to see you. She's, if you can believe it, almost ninety."

And there, when I visited her yesterday afternoon, Persis stood, straight and smiling at the door of her small neat room, furnished with a few familiar pieces from home—a desk, a rug, a chair, a picture or two. She was half the height I remembered, but the voice and the eyes, quietly sizing me up, the smile, were the same. She was, however, no longer the gracious older woman giving me her grown-up advice. Now she was my contemporary. As contemporaries we sat and talked about our families, her grandchildren, her great-grandchildren, friends who survived in Des Moines, and Aunt Flo, her girlhood chum, immured in her luxury flat on the West Coast.

"How is your son?" She had last seen Irving when he was a sturdy youngster of nine. "How are the girls? How is Mary Ellin? How are you?"

One of her own grandsons had just had triplets. Another was a star of sorts on Broadway, and in Hollywood.

We had lunch in the community dining room—roast chicken, stewed fruit and cranberry juice. We then returned to the parlor where she had a cigarette, one of two a day, and opening the French doors, fed her particular squirrel and called my attention to the pleasant outlook, a wide lawn and plantings which in a few months would be a solid wall of blossoms.

Our two hours together were without complaint—she matter-of-factly acknowledged her frailties, her declining eyesight, and the walker needed to get down the settlement's long corridors—but she expressed an absolutely firm interest in her family, my family, and the world around us.

Nor was there anything smarmy in this reasoned acceptance of her lot. She was still an artist. She had had a recent show of her découpages (she no longer felt up to oils). We went through a folder of them—crisp, resourceful, witty compositions both abstract and figurative—tiny slivers of paper which she cut and assembled with a firm hand. Some hung in the corridor on the way to the dining room. Others were for sale in the community gift shop. Another show was planned. The local TV news had scheduled a feature on her work. At nap time I departed.

Seeing Persis as my contemporary, yet remembering her as my mentor, makes me feel neither older nor younger than I should—just better.

. . .

There is a point where life tips. It may come very early for some, very late for others—but one of the glories of wisdom or age or both is that we can see the reasons for accepting life rather than rejecting it. We can see the good in the indifferent—I hesitate to say the bad, for so much that once we would have called *bad* is now indifferent, neutral, and even, on close, steady examination, good. So the gold to be rejoiced in shines there in the midst of the dross. And that is the way it should be for the old. We are the ones whose duty it is, whose joy it should be to recommend life to the cantankerous, carping, complaining young and middle-aged. We are saying, not just that life isn't so bad— or it isn't so bad as you think—but that it is good—it is a privilege, a treasure, not to be wasted, rejected, even for a minute. We old aren't the ones who should be cheered up, cosseted, and cajoled, nor grumpy and glazed in our wheelchairs, wiping the mist from our glasses, brandishing our canes. We should be telling our visitors on their presumed errands of mercy why they really have come—not to buck us up, but to find cheer and courage in our company. The old should be refreshing, not exhausting or depressing. Even *in extremis* they should be giving more than they get, polishing those memorable last words.

I wrote Persis to thank her for lunch and to tell her how heartening my visit had been and how wonderfully cheerful and serene she seemed. Now I want her to write back and ask, "Why, in God's name, shouldn't I be serene and cheerful?" Just that.

Meanwhile, on the radio:

> *Old rockin' chair's got me*
> *Cane by my side*
> *Fetch me that gin, son*
> *'Fore I tan your hide*
> *Can't get from this Cabin,*

Goin' nowhere
Just sit me here grabbin'
At the flies round this rockin' chair.

I hadn't heard the song in half a century and there were the words, a solid block in my memory, in our Water Mill living room. It was as if it were yesterday and the worn 78 was still spinning on the wind-up phonograph in the attic at Forestdale Drive—Mildred Bailey's voice, wispy and true, like some frail woodwind yet to be invented—the needle lifted to play it yet again.

"Marvin," called up the stairs, "Your dinner is getting cold."

—⚶—

MR. DAGMAR WAS TURNED DOWN by the Terence Cardinal Cooke Nursing Home. I guess there was quite a scene when Mr. Sunshine, the admissions officer, told him he was not getting in, although I hadn't had the impression that admission was that important to him. But the rejection obviously made it so.

It is terrible to think that one's applications are still being turned down at ninety as they were for prep school, college, clubs, the service—for bad grades, bad manners, bad teeth—and that the rejection, whether you really care or not, still hurts. It's an indication of some sort of vitality that Mr. D. denies he has.

—⚶—

AN INTERVIEW WITH SALVADOR DALI, now eighty, in his villa in Figueras, Spain, was in the morning *Times*. After months of silence following his wife's death and a fire in which he was severely burned, he decides to speak again. He quotes St. John of the Cross: "Death, come hidden lest I hear you come; the pleasure of dying might give me life."

The newspaper picture shows an old man in a turban with a white upcurved mustache and a tube in his nose. This is the smudged shadow of the once dapper man, black mustache waxed, eyes cagey, whom I interviewed at the St. Regis for *Newsweek* thirty years ago. Dali is still perceptibly snappy, not in appearance, but in words. His explanation for his survival: "I was expelled twice from my family. Each time I emerged victorious. I was expelled twice from the San Fernando Academy of Art, and both times I emerged victorious. I was received by two popes and each time I emerged victorious. I was expelled two times from the Surrealist group, and each time I emerged victorious. Art critics never will be able to understand this enigma, because my life can never be explained, only by painting. Dali, who am I? A hero."

We do not see many examples around us of heroic old age. But—Dali notwithstanding—*heroic* is the wrong word, at least the defiant sort of heroism assigned by the young to the old. Unfortunately the old often accept the estimate of what they are or should be. If old age becomes more commonplace, as it seems to be, that error may be corrected and the real possibilities of old age realized—not as suffering but as blessedness.

And what is that blessedness? It is a realization of the community of human beings, an understanding of others if not yet of God, a respect for God if not yet a love.

Certainly one of the blessings of old age is the expanding realization of the dimension of God's creation and its grandeur, its intricacy, and not only in the physical world, visible and invisible (Dali unquestionably had that) but the moral and spiritual framework, the thought that penetrates and supports it all. The realization which sometimes early in life we grasp as an illuminating flash, should, as we grow old, become a constant vision which each day reinforces. I'd say, not heroics, but common sense.

—m—

IT SNOWED LAST NIGHT in Water Mill, a wonderful wet, clinging snow that is thick on every branch and twig. The porch under the bird feeder is marked by hundreds of finch and sparrow tracks—like the mysterious crackling on the ostrich egg kept in the science cupboard at Callanan Junior High, or the webbed skin of a very old person.

When I took Molly for her midday walk another snow was falling—fine and soft and silent—thick if it can be fine and thick at the same time—falling fast close by, and slowly farther off—an optical illusion.

And above, invisible beyond the snow, the idiot geese are honking, flying in circles, going neither south nor north —released, it would seem, from instinct, from any imperative, indifferent to direction. Like us in the late twentieth century—us, young or old.

PALM BEACH

"BELIEVE ME, the idiot geese have not all stayed behind," I am told by Minda, our closest friend, who has invited us to spend a week with her and her husband Alain. "I would say most of them are still coming south. If you listen you can hear their honking."

Minda and Alain have a small, comfortable house away from the honking, on the shores of Lake Worth, opposite a bird sanctuary, a dense stretch of green that accommodates herons and cranes and many smaller birds, but no geese.

It has been a year since Minda and I went to the Metropolitan Opera to hear *Dialogues of the Carmelites* and in the *entre'acte* discussed our cancers. Since then mine has ostensibly been excised and radiated away at the cost of a temporary death. Hers is being held at bay, barely. The last time I was here, in the spring, just out of the hospital, I was the frail one and Minda was apparently winning her battle. Now our positions seem to be reversed but we don't talk about it.

Instead we visit her mother and aunt, two lively widows who are well past eighty and each winter descend from the north to a vast penthouse, all windows, white sofas and onyx coffee tables with the best security above Miami. We are offered champagne with *pâté*, listen to family talk. They know nothing of Minda's illness. She wants it that way; she would find her mother's and aunt's concern, the old comforting and grieving for the middle-aged, unbearable.

Back at Minda and Alain's house we swim in the pool, play backgammon, watch the news, walk on the beach, go for lunch to Palm Beach's newest and grandest showplace. This is a huge Italianate heap up the road where reality is defeated or at least canceled out in sprawling salons and loggias, an indoor lap pool, a library still uncompleted with one towering wall of morocco-bound ledgers including clips and photo albums of a daughter's wedding in the Montreal Cathedral. These people are rich beyond rich. Later Minda tells us that the husband, once a bus driver, won his wife's, a registered nurse's, hand by closing the bus doors and refusing to open them until she said "yes." Her imprisoned fellow passengers helped convince her. That was thirty years ago.

On home ground, the only outward expression of Minda's sickness is an irritation with the Portuguese butler who is grievously overpaid and can do nothing to please her. She glowers, while he cringes as he circles the table at lunch, at dinner. Otherwise she is her elegant, erudite self, an exemplar of how to set enormous wealth to one side, to be in the midst but not of it.

The intruder in her gut is given no quarter and she refuses any easy disillusionment with all that life has given her and is now threatening to take away.

NEW YORK AND WATER MILL

BERT IS IN DOCTORS' HOSPITAL where he is in cardiac care. When I visit him he is completely in the court of complaint—beginning, middle, and end—against the hospital, the food, the nursing. What swings he manages are within the context of complaint—hostile—dependent—nostalgic—desperate! One wonders what has brought him to such a pass—inviting death, demanding help, but always on his own terms.

Connie S., a friend from earlier, better times who called to discuss Bert's next move urged me to remember that "Bert is an actor," implying that much of his behavior must be seen in that light. How should I respond? By humoring him? Bowing out? How seriously should I take my role in his well-being? That it is a role and one that he more or less writes for me is becoming increasingly clear. At some juncture reality will intrude. If some of the episodes are self-induced—from choice, or, as Connie hinted, the result of drink—where does that leave his caretakers?

Something makes us come back for more. Connie, an old friend; me, relatively new on the scene. And there are others, I hear, who render small services to this old vaudevillian in ruinous condition, but still with the flare that made him a success in whatever he chose to do, now a chair-ridden invalid, a virtuoso of the negligible.

—⚹—

AT ST. JOHN'S, SOUTHAMPTON I was greeted by Mrs. H.—
the oldest member of the congregation. I have long admired
Mrs. H., the relict of a former parson, almost one hundred—
very bright, small, cheerful, smartly dressed, erect in her
forward pew—and at least half a decade older than Bert.
Her children, I understand, are trying to get her to move to
a nursing home in the Middle West. "Very desirable. One
of the best." And—she is firmly resisting.

I would guess one of the greatest gifts we can leave our
children, whether they want it or not, is the memory of us
cheerful up to the lip of the grave—not with that awful pall
of sadness, fear, resentment that can hang, sour and dark,
in the minds of the next generation after we are gone. But
what of the children who refuse to acknowledge the possibility of such a legacy, who demand misery as justification
for their own admirable levelheadedness, their heroic consideration? And what of Mr. Dagmar who has no children
to inspire or victimize: is he depositing a mixed sort of inheritance for his visitors, patient and impatient?

Some other after-church thoughts:

Wisdom can be had in an instant.

We are born wise—ignorance is just the ignoring of
    our birthright.

A misspent life can end in wisdom as well as a
    righteous one.

Innocence is retrievable.

The prodigal can be and often is a grandfather with
    white hair and seamed face, hobbling home.

Jerusalem can be a chair in the window at the
    Southampton Club or a gutter on the Bowery or
    an SRO on upper Broadway.

There is still time to change your mind.

Tell that to Bert—and then duck.

. . .

I am lucky. Because of my physical condition and that
episode at St. Luke's it is possible for me—it is a grace that
has been given to me, and that perhaps I may lose—to look
at each successive day as given for a purpose. Such purpose
is inscrutable maybe, but necessary to consider, to inquire
into. The realization of a purpose and the energy to at least
feebly pursue it have been granted me—not that I am feeble from the residue of sickness but more from the
distractions of a lifetime.

Some days this purpose may seem obvious, other days
obscure. But the possibility of an explanation and even a
solution is always there. The awareness of purpose is one
of the gifts I have been given as a "sort of sick," "sort of
old" person. Along with the very sick and the very old,
the actual perception of life as a gift day by day, not as a
dole, but as a gift, is one that must be shared however awk-
wardly, grudgingly. It is always there, of course, from the
beginning of our lives, but the realization, the acceptance
of it is anything but universal. Young children have it, and
gradually lose it, and then eventually it may come back.
Another reason—*the* reason for living—is for that revelation, that discovery, one of the daily discoveries of old age.

—◊◊◊—

THE BOOK I AM READING, *Number Our Days* by Barbara
Meyrowitz, is a telling piece of social anthropology concerning a community of ancient Jews in Venice, California,
a "double ghetto." This book is the source or perhaps the
follow-up of a memorable documentary film which won a
DuPont Award some years back. In the film I remember
there was a clip of an old woman enumerating the tragedies
of her life to a companion sitting on a bench on the beach.
"Too much, too much," the old man said, but she remained
silent. He could say it, but she wouldn't.

Now, in the book, where he has space to correct himself, the old man on the bench says:

> In old age, we got a chance to find out what a human being is, how we could be worthy of being human. You could find in yourself courage, and know you are vital. Then you're living on a different plane. To do this you got to use your brain, but that's not enough. The brain is combined with the soul. Do you know what I'm talking about? I don't think you could get to this understanding too young, but when you get to it, then you couldn't go before your time, because you are ready . . . I'll tell you how I survive but you won't like it. Every time I say anything about it, people shudder. But you couldn't get away from it, the thing I am talking about. The word is "pain." Pain is the avenue to getting a soul, getting quality from yourself. This is how you get a life that's really on the essence.
>
> You got to go about the pain the right way. You couldn't escape, so you go into it. Then it melts. You get from this the whole thing, the idea of life itself and the result is you're able to take pain in and ignore it because you're so full of living. When you learn to do this—and believe me, it took me a very long time—you get a clarification . . . So when the pain comes, I am patient. I shut up, active silence; I bear it, wait, even overnight, but I mean I bear it. I don't take a tranquilizer, a sleeping pill, some schnapps, or watch television. I stand before it. I call the pain out. After you go through this you discover you got choices. You become whole. This is the task of our life. I want to live this kind of life, so I can be alive every minute. I want to know when I'm awake, I'm altogether awake. When I'm asleep, I'm asleep. It's not masochistic. It's not stoical. In fact, if you want to know, it's Jewish.

One of our prophets said, "In quiet confidence, shall lie your strength."

This statement is from a ninety-year-old man, one of those old men like the ones in Buchenwald marveled at by the teen-age Lusseyran.

As for the old lady, the other person on the bench, she says: "Every morning I wake up in pain. I wiggle my toes. Good. They still obey. I open my eyes. Good. I can see. Everything hurts but I get dressed. I walk down to the ocean. Good. It's still there. Now my day can start. About tomorrow I never know. After all, I'm eighty-nine. I can't live forever."

—◊—

THE OLD BLACK MAN who stands on the corner of 115th and Broadway in front of the University Food Market collecting quarters asked me how I was feeling. I said, "Pretty good—and you?" and he allowed as how he had been troubled by a cold in his back which was better now.

"When we get old we have to expect it, don't we?" he said.

"You don't have to admit that," I said without thinking, automatically resisting being labeled old. However, at the same time I was reaching out and touching his shoulder which was some sort of an admission that what we were in together is not all that bad. Nor did he seem to feel that it was. Cheerful and old, black and old, a panhandler and old.

Georges Braque said, as you grow old, art and life become the same. That is true even if you aren't a master artist, if you are an aging journalist, or an aging panhandler.

But now the uneasy stomach, the insomnia that I said good-bye to, are back, along with the lightheadedness and uncertainty. I am humiliated. Is this the proper way to act for an old person, already a self-proclaimed antique? Or even for one about to be old, lacking only a few weeks of being officially an old person, in other words, sixty-five? Where is the serenity, the understanding, the acceptance, the recognition, the wisdom to which these notebooks I have been filling, these wise men and women I have been consulting, bear witness? Will my confidence, my effrontery return? And yet, this embarrassing lapse into self-pity may be one more proof that I am still alive or that something, a great deal, is left to be done, to be assimilated. That should be neither surprise nor discouragement.

So I have more notes to take, more pages to type of the unwanted journal of my nine months before death which stubbornly I still consider a book. There are more books to be written and to be read, more talks with wife and children, more music to listen to, more church and meetings to attend. And more time to work on my character.

Indeed that there is always more is one of the refreshing discoveries awaiting the old.

If I lack the energy to perfect my tennis game (if I played tennis) or my sonnets (if I wrote them), character still offers me a possibility for improvement. Another chance to clear the passages too often clogged by the years, the passages to reality—mine and the world's I have chosen to inhabit.

If at the end of so many years I still don't ring true, here is the opportunity to reset my pitch. That doesn't mean an uncomfortable frankness with others, but rather tuning out any discord in myself, which is quite a different thing. With this job to accomplish how can anyone say at the end of life there is nothing left to do?

As for insomnia: That prayer is the appropriate and wholesome activity of the aged was brought home again to me last night when I awoke at three and didn't return to sleep until six. At a younger age those hours would have been spent in anxiety over the past, or foreboding for the future, until dawn would work its magic and free me. Now I just pray. Although my prayers soon bring me to an unscalable wall and I don't seem to be able to turn them around and face the open unknown, praying delivers me from time— time as regret, time as dread, time as emptiness and boredom—and the stretch from three to six A.M. seems miraculously short.

It is conceivable—perhaps inevitable—that the reality of God grows upon us with age whether we have been virtu- ous or not, whether we want it or not. If we don't keep pace with His growth within us, His presence becomes a terror, not a blessing. But that terror itself can turn into a blessing at any moment that we choose, for it is our flee- ing, our turning away, our ignoring, that is the terror. God is always the same. As to His bearability, His distance from us, the abyss we perceive between us and God depends on our illusions, nothing more. But the illusions persist.

—◊—

THE PARK AVENUE DOCTOR'S waiting room was full of the elderly getting their prescriptions and leaving—there was no doctor visible, no one invited into the inner chamber; it's obviously some sort of rip-off, a phoney reassurance for the patient, money for the absent doctor. I was there with Bert, complaining as usual, and with good reason. But such petty deceptions are preferable to what is implied in all the discussions of sky-rocketing, uncontainable medical ex- penses, malpractice suits, euthanasia, infanticide, living wills.

What these issues add up to is, Who is worth saving and up to what point? When do you become not worth saving? What are the legitimate dimensions of life? When does life really begin? And when does it really end? How best should it be spent? All these incredibly delicate, difficult questions are being edged into an area where rules, not compassion and hope, will be allowed to decide them.

At what point are the poor, the handicapped, the addicted, the criminal, the hopeless, the old not worth saving? When will they say "Enough" to Bert, to everyone in that uptown waiting room, to the mute ladies and gents before their TV sets in the wards of the nation's nursing homes? When, for these hopeless ones, will simple humanity become too expensive?

But hopeless is a label that can only be applied to ourselves, and there is always something we can do about it. Embedded there between faith and love, hope can be fed from either side.

So be faithful or loving and hope will return. Hope for the poor, the handicapped, the addicted, the criminal, the mad, the old. Hope for oneself. And the numbers, the expense will be no consideration.

—〰—

THIS MORNING WASHING UP IN THE KITCHEN I enjoyed a sinking sensation, a three-dimensional pun springing from the realization that now I probably would never do this or that, accomplish this or that, read this or that, go here or there, meet him or her. And yet if I could, it would mean a distraction from what henceforth should be my increasing concern, my first concern rising through all the bubbles, the curds and the scum. Simplification and concentration by attrition, chosen or imposed, the concern to finally get it right.

But this concern is no reason, no excuse for not keeping on experiencing what one is offered, even to reach out for new experiences. But really new experiences, not fading variations of the old. I want to polish the book on my illness that the editor snooted, and to spend the cash windfall I just received, thanks to my sickness and enforced retirement, on a trip to India and Nepal with Mary Ellin. India with my faulty heart and questionable stomach! Katmandu we find is barely a mile high, well within my heart's limit. If we go to India, PARABOLA Magazine, where I am a senior editor, wants me to interview Father Bede Griffiths, the holy Englishman, at his ashram in Tamil Nadu. Now pushing eighty, he will surely have something to say about age, if not in words, by example.

—ɷ—

MY SIXTY-FIFTH BIRTHDAY. A big party shared with my son Irving, who is about to turn thirty. There are toasts, presents, reassurances from family and friends that I don't "look old."

Mary Ellin quoted her cousin Alice Duer Miller who was the one who said, "Old age is ten years more than your last birthday."

If old age were to be delayed till seventy-five, my chances of making and profiting from it would be proportionately diminished. I'll settle for sixty-five. Still the boundary between middle and old is no more evident than were the equator and the international date line when I crossed them on my way to the South Pacific forty-three years ago. I don't know what I expected then. But suddenly it was yesterday (or was it tomorrow?) and the heat had begun long before, on the dock in San Diego, in the backyard in Des Moines. And out there waiting for me was yesterday, today and tomorrow, all three—hot indeed.

—ɷ—

A VISIT TO BERT AT THE NURSING HOME that finally accepted him. He has gentled down, is quiet, perhaps depressed, reconciled he calls it—giving up.

But wait. The nursing home—he is suddenly emphatic —he cannot stand. It is filled with distressing noises, protests, demands, more so than any normal hospital, noises harder to define or explain or locate. These people here are not supposed to be mortally ill or even very sick. So what are these noises? And as for all the rest, including the man who shares his room, he rejects them as what he calls "retards," not worthy of his attention or company. Fortunately the roommate is deaf. Bert can say anything he wishes to.

—⁂—

MEMORIAL DAY. Minda did not make it out to Water Mill for the long weekend as we had planned. She has gone back to Paris to recover from yet another operation. She is not well, not well at all. "I have survived before."

"Thy will be done," is probably the most frequently repeated phrase in the Christian life—and yet the one that is most difficult to make attractive. We don't want to be the doormat—the dumb cringer waiting for the next blow. But this phrase is definitely there in first place. Perhaps its strength, its appeal, is that instead of a mute passiveness it can indicate a defiance, a daring and challenging. Or even a sort of wild affirmation—I am getting ahead of God, anticipating His wrath, His word, His prodding finger, or an exulting "You have done that—and that—what next? Do Your worst and then let's see."

But need "What God wills" necessarily be unfriendly to our human sense and reason? The way we usually say "Thy will be done" seems to assume catastrophe or at least an apprehensive distaste. We infrequently give God's will credit for the glories—the small daily surprises of life.

This morning, for instance, a perfectly clear blue and

green late May day. We give thanks certainly, when we make the connection. We may even praise God for the sky and the garden under it. But we seldom make the bridge to, the connection with that grim, universally applicable, breathy little aspiration—"Thy will be done."

And you don't even have to go outdoors for your epiphany. Before I got up I was suddenly struck by the beauty of the bedroom ceiling, the beams striped with plaster from the laths that used to be there a century ago. These stripes when I was a little younger reproached me with their presence and challenged me to climb up there and clean them off—a challenge which was never taken. Now they are part of this morning's new vision. Anyone, no matter how old and bed-ridden, can have a ceiling to stare at—or if not a ceiling, the sky.

But how do you apply all this premature wisdom to an absent, sick friend? You can't. You don't.

—⟁—

AN AFTER-CHURCH CONVERSATION with Diana S. about our old houses. She was adding a bath and had hired a Vietnam veteran to do the carpentry. During construction there was a torrential rainstorm and one whole wall fell out. The young man was devastated—he broke down and wept. Diana tried to comfort him by saying philosophically, "Well, we discovered where the leak was." He turned on her fiercely and said, "It is all right for you—you are old. I am young."

When the advantages of "old" become more often acknowledged what will be the effect on the disadvantaged young? There is already a certain amount of grumbling going on about how the old are not so badly off and a movement is afoot to separate them from some of their money and benefits. Maybe envy and resentment will eventually replace guilt and pity in the young's attitude toward the old and won't that be an improvement?

"Age and youth belong together," says Benjamin Mays. "When age is not willing to listen to youth, it has lost its right to leadership. And when youth is not willing to listen to age, it is not ready for responsibility."

—w—

YESTERDAY I AGAIN FELT DIM AND TENSE. I remember twenty years ago, forty years ago, there were dimmer, tenser days, days that I was convinced I couldn't recover from. By now I should know better, but I don't, and the assumption lingers that because of the numbers I am in a natural, irreversible decline. I must acknowledge all to be loss from now on, deterioration of body and mind, dwindling physical and mental capacity. And if the loss isn't conspicuous I will be considered "young for my age," or spry, or remarkably alert and personable.

All that, I know, should be disregarded as irrelevant. As things fall away the core of life is revealed—the tragedy is not that we are being stripped, but that we have waited this long to acknowledge that the stripping is inevitable and now with the process finally under way we are distracting ourselves with pointless regrets rather than marveling at what is being revealed. The same realization made Augustine exclaim at half my age "Late have I loved Thee, oh, beauty both new and old."

But the certainty is lacking.

MINDA DIED IN PARIS ON MONDAY and was buried this morning in Montparnasse Cemetery. A brief paragraph in the *New York Times* revealed her real first name, her other identity under that of the fashionable French baroness, the eldest child of Sam Bronfman, ex-bootlegger, king of Montreal, the founder of a dynasty.

Mary Ellin went over to Europe for the funeral. Minda was sixty. She will never now be "old." But perhaps she didn't need old age. For all her worldliness—and there was no one, I suppose, more worldly than Minda—she had an open, head-on attitude toward life that makes me confident that now she *knows*—that she has ploughed into the light, without cringing, eyes wide open. Her courage, her curiosity, her wit and honesty were always there correcting her course. All the *frou-frou* of her "privileged" life meant little, left her unfazed. Minda at sixty was Minda at twenty-seven, only wiser, surer. It was thirty-five years ago at *Time* magazine, where she was a co-worker who never cashed her pay checks, that she oversaw, advised our difficult, distracted courtship. She was one of the few who saw how and why Mary Ellin Berlin, spoiled and beautiful, and Marvin Barrett, the hick with a veneer, were a possible match, had a future together. She pursued the friendship with us that spanned two continents, two wildly disparate worlds, for more than three decades. And now she is gone.

—∿—

WALKING ON THE BEACH WITH MOLLY. I came upon an old seagull in the sand. It was just short of Tommy Murray's old barn which has now become a million dollar estate, not quite to the point where five years ago Tommy swam into an unfriendly sea and drowned, another friend lost far short of life's designated term. The bird sat above the mark that the strongest wave had made—wings half spread, waiting, I suppose, to die. Not a flutter, not a blink at me, or at Molly when we went by, perhaps a yard away. No sign of alarm, no shudder to indicate that if it were able it would move.

The eye fixed on us was still clear. If we go the same way tomorrow maybe a stronger wave will have pulled the bird out to sea. What was striking about it was not its weakness, its inability to flap away, but its stillness and repose there at the edge of a treacherous ocean, the clear eye at the edge of its doom.

Our house is suddenly cheerful, full of the young and their concerns. Katherine and Benjy Swett, her long-time boyfriend, have joined us with their current project, *The Insight Guide to Italy.* We are all put to work. Katherine, the book's editor, is writing the section on Rome herself. Benjy is finishing up Apulia. Mary Ellin is reading the manuscript for possible errors. I have been enlisted to brighten up the section on the Veneto. Our typewriters and our memories of Italy are all being put to use.

Meanwhile Mary Ellin and I are making arrangements for our trip to India, packing our summer clothes although here autumn is moving in.

INDIA

PONDICHERRY. SIX A.M. The sunrise over the Bay of Bengal is very pink—enough pink in the sky to furnish India, a nation partial to that color, its allotment for years to come. Three rickshaws are waiting in the alley under our balcony—the bleating goat that woke me is silent—the sea is loud.

An Indian family out on the lawn is staring at the dawn along with me. On the water, barely visible in and out of the troughs of the waves, are maybe a half-dozen two-man boats pulling out onto the bay, with the rowers facing each other in their fragile craft. A low false ceiling of wispy clouds lies in a strip above the water with a bright hole in it where the sun is about to appear. Higher up the pink is seeping out of a clear blue sky.

Is this the dawn that "comes up like thunder out of China 'cross the bay" that Poppa used to sing about in the parlor at 1408 Forestdale, with Cousin Nellie in her Sunday hat accompanying him ?

And what exactly is *across the bay*? Certainly not China. The Andaman and Nicobar Islands? Burma? The mouths of the Irrawaddy? The old Moulmein pagoda? All of them and on beyond—Sumatra, Singapore, the magical, mysterious East as Kipling and Poppa would have it.

That this trip to India, three weeks in the north with a tour, a week on our own in the south, is an interruption, not a distraction from growing old, is more and more apparent. It is a space inserted, lifted out of the sequence of our lives—bearing some relation to what has gone before, but so far not much.

Mary Ellin says it reminds her of Italy—the prehistoric and the antique ruins alongside the sixteenth century riches, with an overlay of the tacky and modern; there is a sense of history from the very beginning. I see no resemblance really to anything, or if I do, it is almost immediately canceled out by a shadow, a silhouette that is totally apart—a building, a figure in native costume, an oddly shaped hill rising out of nowhere.

Nothing is as we imagined it would be. Perhaps the Taj Mahal. But no, not even the Taj Mahal. Our imaginations in that instance failed us. Our skepticism was defeated. A lifetime of postcards and calendars confirmed and instantly obliterated. Or Fatehpur Sikri—the abandoned city that sits on a dry table of land outside Agra. We hadn't even imagined that, or known it existed. It is there all of a piece—

rose red with its huge portal and the wildly ironic words inscribed on its lintel in alien characters already translated and firmly set in my memory: "The world is a bridge—cross over it but build no house upon it." Suddenly these memorable words, ascribed to Christ, the words which I chose to ignore half a lifetime ago, are emblazoned up there, written against the sky. And when did Jesus say them, and to whom? They are in no gospel, no concordance that I know of, for all their authentic ring, particularly ringing when Gerald Heard spoke them in the upper cloister at Trabuco, his brand-new California headquarters, without attribution, as if they might have been his own.

Yesterday we went to Arunachala, the holy mountain with its singular profile and under it Ramana Maharshi's frumpy little ashram, dusty, nearly deserted but still authentic. We were permitted to see the room where the great soul meditated and I presume received Somerset Maugham, an encounter which furnished the climax and the *raison d'etre* for *The Razor's Edge*, and, I would guess, for the rest of Maugham's life. Maugham was still talking about the Maharshi and human liberation beside George Cukor's swimming pool in Beverly Hills the year he stood on his head and, upside down, drank a glass of water, a yoga trick, at a party where Mary Ellin, just turned eighteen, was a silent amazed witness.

There was a garlanded couch with a large tinted photograph of the Maharshi propped on it—covered with red plush—not the tiger skin that Maugham reported. An Indian lady in a sari sat meditating opposite. She didn't open her eyes at our rustling, whispering presence. The room was small and dark—no effulgence here. We were too late for lunch with the devotees. "Thank God," said Mary Ellin. The ashram bookstore was open, with people in white sheets puttering about, the relicts of the great teacher, but not in an officious way. The whole atmosphere was apart, separated from touring strangers.

From the top of the Indian subcontinent downward we have encountered many holy places—the temple north of Katmandu with the great eye and the circle of tinkling prayer wheels and the lamas in robes the color of dried blood; the naughty temples of Khajuraho, sex reduced to decoration, to theological formulae; Elephanta with its impossible-to-contradict statements, the tangled trinity, the singular, upward thrusting God. Ellora, Ajanta, Mahabalipuram, all impart their own message about life, about reality. At the temple in Tiruvannamalai we visited an anchorite in his grubby cell in a wall—no smiles, no words, a silent blessing in exchange for our offering of a few rupees left in a soda can, at his elbow a big American alarm clock. An elephant, inexplicably healthy and sleek, was chained to a pillar opposite his door—Ganesh. In India there is a god everywhere. A god and poverty.

There were the outstretched hands and bowls outside the beige and ochre observatory at Jaipur, reaching up to us as we mounted the not-so-sleek elephants, to climb to the fortress-palace at Amber, reaching out to the litter that carried me up the long steps to the temple caves of Ajanta. We had been advised not to fill (but had anyway) the beggars' strong brown hands, evidence of a poverty so general and disregarded that its meaning was unreadable.

By the time we had reached South India we were almost grasping it. Those people stopping in the fields, standing by their goats or their cattle, in front of thatched mud huts, driving their flocks of ducks along the road, in the bright saris, spreading their grain on the macadam to be threshed by the immense, square, roaring, rushing, mile-devouring Ashok Leyland lorries. Turning to observe us, the intruders in our ancient Mercedes, their dark eyes showed no hostility, no more curiosity than the camera shutter we aimed at them.

Now the sun is up, rising above the clouds full force, blinding me standing opposite it on the hotel balcony. Two bats flap inland, wheeling away from the light. A man is brushing his teeth next to the wall. There is much teeth brushing in India and the teeth, regular, white in the dark, handsome faces, show it.

The boats out on the water are putting up sails now, some grey, some white. A raven lands on the sill above me, looking down, scolding. In the alley our driver in a T-shirt and sarong, who chose to spend the night in his car, is now out washing it.

And where are the old people in India? Why am I not registering them? Does the climate dispose of them? Have they all taken to the woods? Even in Benares there was no sense of their presence, or for that matter, their absence.

—m—

THE ASHRAM OF SHANTIVANAM, our destination in the south, a short ride north from Trichy, is filled with young people presided over by Bede Griffiths, who *is* old. No holy mountain overshadows us. Through a grove beyond the main settlement there is a holy river, the Cauvery, wide and slow flowing. Shantivanam is what the Trabuco community might have become had the group members hung on, had they exchanged Southern California for the bottom of India. But here Mary Ellin and I sleep on cement beds and eat what to our western palates seems truly disgusting food.

Father Griffiths was fifty when he left his Benedictine monastery in England in favor of a dying community in southern India. He is now, two communities later, in his eightieth year. He wears a sanyassin's ochre robe which leaves his chest bare; he has a beard, long white hair, and the large well-defined features of an upper-class Englishman with an expression of, if not amused, tolerant attention.

The ashram compound, a dozen multicolor buildings set in the green shade, includes a manger with half a dozen cows, an open refectory, an octagonal verandahed library, and a chapel conforming in style to the temples we have been visiting, topped by a four-sided pyramid where the colorfully glazed figures are Christian saints. Griffiths' hut is small and sparely furnished. He speaks in a soft, modulated Oxford English. He was C. S. Lewis' tutee when they were both unbelievers.

In answer to some question of mine—I am there, after all, to question him—he says, "I see faith as awakening to the transcendent. In the Christian perspective we say God is beyond the reason, beyond the created world altogether, and it's necessary to open the heart and the mind to the transcendent. Normally the transcendent manifests through some particular tradition. This seems to be where the religions differ. If you awaken to it in the Buddhist tradition you name it Nirvana and you enter into the Eightfold Noble Path and so on. And if you're a Hindu you name it Brahman or Atman and take the path of yoga, and if you're a Christian you name it God the Father and you enter into the path of Christ. So each is a path to the Supreme having its own unique character."

And again, "This awakening can take place under any circumstance and does so. But if it's to be nourished and to grow, most people need a time apart. And many need not only a time but a life. A monastery or an ashram is a place which exists precisely to enable people both to awaken and to grow in their awareness of the transcendent."

The year could be 1942 instead of 1985, the place Southern California not Southern India, the bearded man Gerald Heard not Bede Griffiths, me, a provisional naval ensign AWOL for a weekend in search of enlightenment, not the aging father of four grown children on a month off. "If you have been privileged to see the truth or even suspect it," Gerald had told me, giving me credit for a conviction I didn't yet possess, "you are obliged to act on that suspicion. There is no turning back. Once you see the worms at the banquet creeping up the table cloth . . ."

Indeed it has been nearly a half a century since I have had a conversation like this—naked, unashamed, unembarrassed, with someone who admittedly knows much more than I do, has taken chances I have yet to take—about God and how to get to Him. Then it was Gerald speaking in the same varsity accent, with the same precision, the same emphasis—his beard red, not white, no sanyassin's robe, a denim jacket, jeans before they were the fashion, his thin elegant hand demonstrating evolution's gift of the opposable thumb, his palm rejecting the world, his fingers beckoning in the horizon, the hills, God's whole creation— me. The same vision—the same recommendations—the same choice.

"Beyond the body is the spirit," says the man in the ochre robe, "another dimension where we go beyond the mind, the senses, and the feelings, and we're aware of the transcendent reality; and that is the goal of life, to get to that."

I shiver. A young man in California, an old man in India. The same shiver.

At what point did this trip to India change from being a vacation with my chic, intelligent, responsive fifty-eight-year-old wife, an extended semi-serious lark perhaps if at sixty-five one is capable of larking, to a pilgrimage? It was the moment I recognized what I was up to and made the connection with what I had done before and told myself this must be a pilgrimage, the second of my life, acknowledging at the same time that the whole thing, all life, must be considered a pilgrimage. And even the dismally familiar should become on each successive day as disturbing, as challenging as the turrets of the Taj Mahal, the long shadow of Arunachala, or Akbar's towering portal.

On a walk by the river some distance from the ashram I was overtaken by the hammer-heavy irony of that inscription on the largest gate in India rising beyond the sprawling courtyards of Fatehpur Sikri on their vast platform above the waterless Indian plain. There it had stood in immense arching letters at the top of its broad flight of steps—the culmination of one of the most striking and futile feats of monument building in history, deserted after thirteen years by the mighty Akbar who had intended his palace to house sages from at least four great traditions in inappropriate splendor. Could Akbar the Great, with his greed for truth, for explanations, permit himself such an expensive joke? Such an enormous irony? He could and did.

And what of Gerald who had spent his inheritance on his lovingly detailed retreat on a sunburnt California hill to house himself and a dozen like-minded young companions, who would desert it in less than a decade? When he quoted Akbar quoting Jesus, did he anticipate the irony, the impending parallel? I am not at all sure he did.

On the flight from Bombay to Paris, under a full moon, there, as on a map, exactly as on a map, lay the whole of Arabia—the shape of a butcher's cleaver, the shape of life, of the imagination. If you get high enough and look down and ahead, there Arabia lies spread out under you—with Africa dark beyond.

NEW YORK

IN MANHATTAN, UNLIKE BENARES, the streets are filled with the old. Among these wanderers without apparent destination, these dodderers who know too well where they are heading, this afternoon, after visiting Bert, while waiting for the crosstown bus, and leaning wearily against the shelter support—it was a long wait—I saw Christ.

It was a very simple, sharp vision. Coming toward me across the intersection, an old man in a grey raincoat and a stitched narrow-brimmed cloth hat lost his footing, slipped and fell to the pavement. He was not close enough so that my instant reflex was to reach out and pick him up, not as close as the man who was bending over and touching him, nor as near as the girl in green who had made a gesture in his direction and after a moment, looking anxiously at the light that was about to change, kept on walking. For me, there was a gap, a moment of reticence, of unworthiness, and then I ran out. Between us, the other man and I got the old man to his feet. For a minute he seemed limp—at least resistant to being helped—and I observed to myself that his dead weight, which I was struggling to get upright, certainly represented a great deal more than the fifteen pounds allowed me by my cardiologist.

Somehow the two of us steered him to the curb. The street was strangely silent. There was no honking, no expression of impatience from cabbies or truck drivers or people in sports cars leaning out of their windows, urging us to clear the way.

Once we got him to the curb and standing shakily, traffic resumed. The other helper, assuring himself that the old man was ambulatory and that I was willing to take over, moved on. So I was left with a trembling grey-haired man with two brutally scraped and bleeding hands and a great bleeding lump on his forehead which he was trying to cover with his hat. There had been a cheap black-bean rosary beside him on the street which I had picked up and stuffed into his pocket as I pulled him to his feet. He was clutching some crumpled bills in one hand, and in the other, a bright yellow plastic bag obscenely stretched by what turned out to be a half gallon of cream sherry, miraculously unbroken (the reason he was out in the first place, or one reason although there was no telltale smell of liquor on his breath).

I asked him where he lived, and he reluctantly—"they mustn't know about this"—admitted residence in another, fancier nursing home a few blocks away.

I volunteered to take him there by taxi but, no, he said, he would prefer to walk. He said he was missing his cane which he believed he left in the liquor store off the corner where he had bought the sherry. He hadn't. The young man at the cash register said, yes, he had been there not too long before but had left nothing behind. We looked along the counter and by the door. The young man gave me his card and asked with a distressed look in the old man's direction if there was anything else he could do. There obviously wasn't.

And so, the taxi once more refused, we tottered off down Third Avenue, Christ and I, heading for another liquor store where he'd made his first visit and decided he could do better on the price. Indeed he had saved twenty or twenty-five cents, he said bitterly.

We talked as we walked and I heard only some of his answers, spoken in a hesitant murmur. He came from Cazenovia in upstate New York. He had a brother in Syracuse. He had been at the home for almost ten years. I revised my estimate of his age upward. What had he done before? He said something about the Christian brothers— whether he was one or simply lived with them, I couldn't make out. His mother had been forty-five when he was born. He had had a sister who died of erysipelas. That was about it. He had a fit of trembling, then wanted to know how his forehead looked. Did it show? I tried to wipe the blood off but it kept coming. The angry knob was growing on his right temple. We pulled his hat still lower on his brow to cover it.

I offered a taxi again—a doctor—we could go to the hospital down the avenue. He refused with an emphasis reinforced by panic and stood straighter to demonstrate his recovery. We finally came to the liquor store he had visited earlier. I waited outside with the yellow plastic bag while he went in (he didn't want them to know that he had made his purchase elsewhere). No sign of the cane.

We went on another block or two, and avoiding the front entrance of the nursing home, rang the bell at the back door. Eventually someone came—an Irish attendant, not uniformed. He asked what had happened, where Francis —that was his name—had been; he wasn't critical, but concerned. They had been worried. Francis asked to go to his room on thirteen and he wanted me to take him. No nonsense about the thirteenth floor being the fourteenth at this last stop before eternity. So I took him up to thirteen, past the expressions of tactful concern along the way, past the doors, open and shut, where other men and women, older and frailer, were waiting like Francis in a place that was quieter than a hospital, cleaner and brighter than an SRO hotel, for what came next.

He had a single room with bath, simple and comfortable, with a crucifix over the bed, holy pictures on the walls. He wanted to give me something for my trouble, groped in his pocket. I tried to tell him as gently as possible that it had been my pleasure, my opportunity to come to his assistance, that he had already given me much more than I deserved. But how do you tell Christ that he is Christ? You don't. You just consider the times you have been Christ yourself in the past and will be in the future, squeeze his shoulder in a gesture of reassurance, and close the door gently behind you, leaving him sitting there on the edge of his bed still wearing his blood-stained hat.

"What water flowing by is, so is our life and everything happening in it," wrote the Russian Orthodox St. Tikhon of Zadonak. "We see that water in the river flows unceasingly and passes by and everything floating upon the water, like wood or refuse, likewise passes by. Some years ago I did not exist and behold I am in the world like other creatures . . . I was a baby and this passed by. I was an adolescent and this passed by. I was a youth and this left me. I was a mature and strong man, and I am no more. Now my hair is white and I am weary with old age but this is also passing by. I approach my end and I will go the way of all flesh. I was born in order to die. I die in order to live. 'Remember me, O lord, in your Kingdom.'"

I walked this morning in the park along the river, New York's river, and it was suddenly every walk I'd ever taken. I eat and sleep and it is the same. I am walking, eating, sleeping, outside, against time; for every day in my life I am, I always have been, I for the moment know, in the Kingdom.

1986

1986

THERE IS A PICTURE of me as an infant in Des Moines sitting on my great-grandfather Bartram Galbraith's lap. Perhaps eight months old, I am staring up into that wonderful, white, untrimmed beard which reached to the third button of his shirt (I am all in white myself, in a lovely hand-embroidered white baby dress)—the old man, the prairie pioneer, the retired blacksmith, his backlit head all light—my little face shining, tilted upward towards his. Some clever relation had put me there saying, "Hold him, Grandpa. Hold little Bartram. Hold it!" And we are caught forever—staring with amazement at each other.

Actually it was my brother on Great-grandpa Galbraith's lap. I found that out only recently—too late to ever believe it. My father's maternal grandfather was dead before I was born and I had his name for less than a month. Then Grandfather Barrett who was alive and stubborn insisted I be named for *his* father, Marvin Barrett, the pioneer Michigan farmer dead before any of his grandchildren or great-grandchildren had laid eyes on him. That blessed baby in the picture was my brother Dirk, named for Grandfather Kruidenier, my mother's father.

Brother Dirk a decade later was also privileged to lay eyes on the original Marvin Barrett's widow, Great-grandmother Helen, before she tripped over a rocker and died in her hundredth year. On that important visit, I, her husband's namesake, was left at home, victim of some fleeting childhood sickness. So it was Dirk who saw her in her Richland, Michigan kitchen—by then she seldom left it—and got her blessing. I have the cherry-wood drop-leaf table she sat at. It is behind me in our Water Mill library as I write—but without the memory, the loving caress.

Still, Helen's story is one that I have made mine, that everyone loves—my children, my in-laws, anyone who gives me the time of day to tell it. It is a story that stretches beyond old age in both directions, two lives spanning a young nation's history and pointing to its future.

Helen was born in Painted Post, in upstate New York in 1830, the twenty-seventh of twenty-seven children. Her father, John Dolson, was seventy-nine, old enough to have crossed the Delaware with George Washington, to have fought at the battle of Trenton and witnessed the surrender of Cornwallis at Yorktown. Seventeen seventy-six was close enough to touch, to kiss, to have your hand grasped by. At least if you were brother Dirk.

At thirteen, Helen, by then an orphan, had with her older sister Sophia found her way to Five Points in Manhattan, the notorious haunt of thugs and prostitutes, and somehow escaped by her fourteenth birthday westward as an indentured servant. Within the year she was a farmer's bride in the new state of Michigan, bearing nine children, dying herself in 1930 the year after Dirk's visit. Two generations adding up to 178 years.

She rated a *Time* magazine obit.

DIED. Mrs. Helen M. Barrett, ninety-nine, one of nine living daughters of Revolutionary War soldiers, of old age; at Richland, Mich. Her father, soldier Johannes Van Dolson served under General Washington at

Trenton, at Yorktown, had nine children by each of three wives, had her when he was aged seventy-eight. When first married, she spun and wove her children's clothes; baked, made soap, candles over a hearth fire. [A few mistakes, but no more than usual.]

And now, having seen the others, Helen's sons and daughters, grandsons and granddaughters grow old and die, we—my brother Dirk and I—no matter which of us was that blessed baby on Great Grandpa Galbraith's lap—are old ourselves.

—ᴍ—

ACCORDING TO THE *NEW YORK TIMES*, the 1980 census showed 2,492,157 people in the U.S. were in institutions, of them 1,426,371 in homes for the aged. In 1970, 928,000 were in homes for the aged, in 1960, 470,000—these figures evidence of the phenomenal increase in stockpiling and isolating the elderly.

As I recall in the 1920s and 1930s living in the Home for the Aged, a solid two story brick building out from the center of Des Moines, was considered neither a privilege nor a misfortune. In late spring, frail, white-haired ladies in long white dresses with high collars strolled unselfconsciously on the front lawn with their visitors, and old gentlemen in panamas with canes, the same. What at that time was to be avoided at all costs was the county home, otherwise known as "the poor farm," where you were sent to be forgotten. This, I fear, is what today's old folks' homes in most cases resemble, even the fanciest. Being old back then was nothing necessarily to complain about, to apologize for, or fight against. I can't recall one murmuring word about being old from any of those ancient relatives of mine, not even Will Galbraith, our poverty-stricken great uncle. He kept a room in a flea-bag hotel off Mulberry Street in downtown Des Moines and attended one family dinner in three, shocking us with his stories of the raffish folks he gossiped with in his threadbare lobby. He had a cane, and a stiffened leg which he was forever adjusting (from a train accident in his late middle age; he was too young for the Civil War, too old for the Spanish-American). He gave up the ghost one day when I was away at Harvard or World War II, and was planted in Greenwood, the pioneers' cemetery downtown, in the Galbraith plot alongside the old man with the white beard, his father.

So how is it living in an old folks home today? The ladies I visit in the Southampton Nursing Home propose four answers.

Edna—uncomplaining, cheerful, in the bed closest to the window. She tells me about her nephews and her friends, and about herself; at one time she was a supervisor of nurses. Last December she opened all the windows in the Advent card the day I brought it. She can, her caretakers tell me, be a real devil.

Augusta—always sleeping in her chair—dressed. Only once in dozens of visits have I seen her standing, indecisive, in the middle of her room. The TV set is always on —unattended. Augusta wakes gently, responds, says she is fine or not so fine—she answers questions but offers nothing of her own—she receives what I bring, whether flowers or a holiday card, graciously, with a beautiful smile. Since she has nothing to say I fill the silence with my own family news—Mary Ellin Jr.'s new job at *USA Weekend* has taken her to Washington, Katherine is engaged, Elizabeth and Sasha have moved to Los Angeles.

Mrs. Jolliffe—about to be ninety. Frequently out when I call, out playing cards, visiting friends, looking in on the young men who have taken her house on Cobb Road, or having lunch at a local bar. Mrs. Jolliffe accepts my presents with appropriate comments: "How lovely! How amusing." As I leave she turns back to the letter-writing my arrival has interrupted.

Mrs. Batchelder—one hundred and seven, older than anyone I have ever known. Until last year, according to Malcolm, our rector, she was alert, telling stories about England in Queen Victoria's day. But she is now blind, frail almost to the point of invisibility. She gives me her tiny hand. On my next to the last visit to her I talked about the Murray children whose nurse she once was—they are now old folks themselves, the ones who have survived. On the last visit we talked about the Murray children's children— all grown. This time there is no gossip. Just prayers. "Yes," she says with a girlish eagerness. "That's what I'd like—a prayer." And when I've read it, "Beautiful," she says. "That was a long one." She permits me to press her hand again in farewell.

—m—

DEATHBED CONVERSIONS may be more frequent than we think. Malcolm told me of a man who had died the previous Monday. I had visited this gentleman two Sundays ago in the hospital (visits to the hospital on Sunday, and to the old folks mid-week, are my country good works). He apparently had for two years a series of infections that no one understood or could treat. When I stood by his bed offering him a prayer he was gasping for breath. He had been a crucifer at St. John's fifty years ago, Malcolm said, and had left the church before confirmation when he had not been assigned to carry the cross at the funeral of Reverend Fish, the church's aged first rector. For half a century he had been an unbelieving school custodian. Malcolm had anointed him and given him the final rites. The man said if by some miracle he survived he would come back to St. John's and finally be confirmed.

I find such late life turnarounds heartening, whether it is a school janitor or Sir Kenneth Clark. In his autobiography he gives a possible explanation for his own last minute return to the church, a return which had startled his worldly friends.

"I lived in solitude in Bernard Berenson's villino surrounded by books on the history of religion, which have always been my favorite reading," Clark recalled. "This may help to account for a curious episode that took place on one of my stays in the villino. I had a religious experience. It took place in the Church of San Lorenzo, but did not seem to be connected with the harmonious beauty of the architecture. I can only say that for a few minutes my whole being was irradiated by a kind of heavenly joy, far more intense than anything I had known before. This state of mind lasted for several months, and, wonderful though it was, it posed an awkward problem in terms of action. My life was far from blameless: I would have to reform. My family would think I was going mad, and perhaps, after all, it *was* a delusion, for I was in every way unworthy of receiving such a flood of grace. Gradually the effect wore off, and I made no effort to retain it. I think I was right; I was too deeply embedded in the world to change course. But that I had felt "the finger of God" I am quite sure, and, although the memory of this experience has faded, it still helps me to understand the joys of the saints."

It obviously hadn't faded, just gone underground to reappear at the end of his long life. Along with the school custodian Clark gives proof that however frivolous or bullheaded our reasons for delay, we can be given a second chance. If many are called, and few chosen, the few chosen may include the twice called, and in the nick of time.

It seems apparent that as we grow older our negotiations with God under any circumstances must grow more delicate, more exact—like a captain making home port who must be ever more precise in his conning as he approaches his destination. Far at sea we can be indifferent to finer reckonings. But close to shore small mistakes can be fatal—if anything can be fatal where every rock and shoal, set and drift is God.

"For Thou art there where seeing is one with being seen, and hearing with being heard, and tasting with being tasted, and touching with being touched, and speaking with hearing, and creating with speaking," said Nicolas of Cusa, very close to his own mooring.

NEW YORK

SPRING, IF YOU AGREE WITH T. S. ELIOT, is a hard time for all of us, young and old. Yesterday after a morning working on my book on sickness, I visited Bert, who had been transferred from his double room in the nursing home to an open ward in Cabrini Hospital where, already skin and bones, he was dramatically reduced. A tube in his nose—no teeth—his tongue was lolling out of his mouth—his eyes seemed much smaller but alive in contact. In this large room filled with strangers, plugged into strange equipment, he indicated he doesn't know where he is—but he knows me.

I talked to him, as usual, about what is going on in my own life—plans for my daughter Katherine's wedding—the engagement party last night given by her Aunt Elizabeth and Uncle Alton, the Sunday lunch in Westchester to meet the groom's family and friends, the program on TV celebrating the upcoming ninety-eighth birthday of my father-in-law, older even than Bert. How great it was. "I know," Bert said, suddenly alert, the mention of show business celebrity rousing him. "I watched. Even President Reagan was good—the only good thing he has said in months." There was the unexpected humor, the wicked glint which I hadn't seen in a long time. There were none of the usual complaints about his eyes, his teeth, the doctor, what life has done to him.

"How is the food?" I asked him. "It can't be as good even as at the place uptown." To this he agreed, barely audible now. I held his hand. I told him we were praying for him at the Cathedral and thinking of him at home. I sent him Mary Ellin's love. I reminded him of how long he and I have been friends. How long *had* it been since I first visited him surrounded by his mementos in his single room occupancy hotel on Upper Broadway? Six years? I was not certain. All of this he agreed to gently. Finally I stood and told him I'd be back.

A moment after I got home from the hospital the phone rang. It was Mr. Berlin for Mary Ellin. At first I didn't recognize his voice. It was softer—not sweeter necessarily but without the characteristic rasp. Not that what he was calling to say was particularly soft. He was calling to complain about the length of the letter that Mary Ellin had written him about the birthday program. He couldn't read it; his eyes were that much worse; Mrs. Berlin wasn't well enough to read it to him; he had to ask the nurse to read it.

The message, the real message, was that Mrs. B. could no longer run interference for him, that he was now the comparatively well one, at ninety-eight caring for his ailing eighty-three-year-old wife. After her last visit Mary Ellin had reported her mother sitting in her wrapper in the library saying very little, listening to the news of the children but scarcely talking herself—she who for most of her life was in charge of any conversation.

Now, for all the birthday communications, dozens of letters from old acquaintances and fans, there was a painful sense of isolation and beyond that the seeming contradiction of basically wanting to be left alone. The two of them against the world, after sixty years of marriage, propping each other up, is a formidable and touching demonstration of world-class fidelity. You want to help but you aren't permitted. And the sounds they make are not always comfortable to the ear. This prompts a question. Where, now, will the help come from?

"If you don't believe in God when you are ninety," Mr. B., the lifelong agnostic, had told his devout Catholic wife a decade back, "you are a fool." But no such declaration had been reported lately.

By the time Mary Ellin returned her father's call he had calmed down. "I think he was making an editorial comment," she said when she hung up, "that I am getting a little long-winded."

Is it your children or your parents who teach you about life, death, sickness, and unrequited—or requited—love. Your children are like sleepwalkers on some perilous roof; you—their host, their caretaker—dare not wake them, knowing that to survive they must wake themselves. Your parents—behind glass—are inaccessible still, understood or appreciated just a little too late; they are your caretakers, your hosts. If you are lucky, like Mary Ellin (my own parents, half-appreciated, half-understood, are long since dead), you grasp both roles, set them side by side like a stereopticon slide to achieve a new, more real dimension.

. . .

Tonight we went to *Falstaff*—an old man's opera. After the opera Mary Ellin said she hoped that my book would include examples of the remarkable old, Verdi and *Falstaff* being the immediate occasion for the comment. She included in this category Max L., who at eighty-four is battling two or three cancers, a wavering heart, and yet is embarking on another major book as well as maintaining all his other activities.

But to display the continuing accomplishments of the genius old, I responded, is not my purpose. The point is to discover that underlayer of skills and accomplishments that the remarkable old share with the unremarkable old. Not to boast about Verdi's *Falstaff,* or Monet's *Water Lilies,* or Michelangelo's last *Pieta,* or Picasso's *Tauromachia,* or the last works of Goya, or Rembrandt's final self-portrait. These indeed are amazing and inspiring, perhaps even disquieting, but more immediately and continually useful to us as we age are possibilities that grow instead of diminish, that are preparations rather than rear-guard actions however magnificent. Besides, in these accomplishments of the famous old we must look for not only amazing expertise but for marks of wisdom, and if we look hard enough perhaps we shall find them.

—⚊⚊—

TRYING TO DO GOOD HERE AND THERE is not such a cop-out as some latter-day critics would have it. "The surest method of arriving at a knowledge of God's eternal purposes about us is to be found in the right use of the present moment. God's will does not come to us in the whole, but in fragments, and generally in small fragments. It is our business to piece it together, and to live it into one orderly vocation." I agree with Father Faber. My grasping of life, such as it is, has always been in fragments, by intuitions, insights, inklings—not by systems, rules, facts. The questions is, Are the fragments truly significant, are the intuitions valid? Even when I am confronted by a rigid system I try to dismantle it, like a monkey, restless, in search of something asymmetrical. I swarmed through Gerald's system in search of those anomalies, those odd shapes. It is why I prefer Christ's teachings to St. Paul's, notwithstanding that uncharacteristic hymn to charity; Lao Tsu's and Rumi's off-center stabs to the Buddha's and Mohammed's balanced precepts. The system is there, hidden and demanding, but it is the intuition that gives it conviction and life.

So, in a slapdash, extemporizing way I have tried to use the present moment to do good—be good. In order to do good you must be good, in order to be good you must do good—it's the chicken or the egg—a draw.

Consequently I have visited Mrs. Batchelder and the ladies at the nursing home, bringing my offering of prayers and, when they are blooming in the field behind our house, of flowers. I visit the sick and dying Episcopalians in Southampton Hospital. I took on Mr. Dagmar for the West Side Mission to the Elderly. Before that I gave a quorum of nuns a regular lift from the South Bronx to the old people in Jersey City, with room left over in the back of my station wagon for the cut-rate fruits and vegetables they picked up on the Jersey side for the South Bronx foodless and homeless.

"What old people? What nuns?" What was I, a derelict Presbyterian, an about-to-be Episcopalian, doing giving rides to a carful of young women in blue-bordered white saris telling beads?

Somewhere on the upper East Side, sometime in the Seventies, Mother Teresa, a wrinkled lady in the same white and blue sari, on leave from India, asked for volunteers, people who drove, who had cars to drive. Once you made eye contact with Mother Teresa you did what she asked. The next Sunday I picked up the nuns at their South Bronx tenement and drove them to Jersey City where in a tall, dark building on a bluff the old folks waited—"boys" on one floor, "girls" on another—for their cookies, tangerines, apples, and cigarettes, to have their fingernails cut, their hair combed, their hands held, their prayers said. From there it was back to the Bronx and the kids so under-privileged they didn't know how to play properly and the shut-ins, ancient ladies in tiny tenement cubicles caring for the next generation but one, willing to be civil to any interloper the nuns might drag along. And finally offering coffee and sandwiches to the men and women (who could tell if they were young or old?), the "instant" elderly, huddled up and down the steps of the midtown terminals, the last stop for them and their bursting bundles, half of them turning their faces to the wall till we passed by. "Doing good." I wondered, when I paused long enough to consider, who was doing what to whom? And why were the objects of my visitation, my fragments as Father Faber would have them, always or almost always old?

WATER MILL

THE MASSIVE PREPARATIONS for Katherine and Benjy's wedding have little to do with old age. Three days of cooking, Mary Ellin, her sister Elizabeth, Mrs. Lodi, our housekeeper and friend, all in the kitchen, early and late, me sent off on a dozen errands—to the grocers, the rental place, the liquor store. The big yellow and white tent is finally pitched in the back yard. The tables and chairs are set up, the dance floor designated, two dozen vases put out for our neighbor Jessie Wood to fill with flowers.

We have had the rehearsal in the little red church by the sea, shingled and gabled, with its miniature stained glass windows, its old rugged pews set facing each other at the crossing, its sailors' mementos (it was once headquarters for a Coast Guard unit), the plaques honoring the summer people who have come here to worship in their blazers and flannels, their linen dresses, every July and August for three-quarters of a century.

The bridal dinner presided over by Shiela and Steve Swett has been held in the quaint building that is no longer used as the Water Mill train station, now a fashionable restaurant.

Following the excitement of the endless arrangements for cars, dress, the veil of family lace, the initials spelled out in sweet alyssum by the driveway, comes the tear-jerking beauty of the moment. The walk down the aisle, me with the young bride, her sister Mary Ellin behind us; our old friend Henry Sturtevant, the wayward rector of St. Clements, waiting at the altar; the two young people kneeling introduced by the older sister Elizabeth's strong, flawless reading of those inevitable words: "Though I speak with the tongues of men and of angels and have not charity, I am become as sounding brass, or a tinkling cymbal," the apostle Paul's hymn to love, King James version, launching them onto the sea of life. Is that it? As hackneyed as that? All of us for one moment looking forward, age forgotten.

The young people have gone on their cross-country honeymoon. The tent is struck, the tables and chairs are folded and carried away, the dance floor is dismantled, and the garden, untended for a week, is in need of watering and weeding.

—◊◊◊—

At the nursing home Mrs. Batchelder is withdrawing, and when you are one hundred and seven there is little space to retreat or advance into. On my last visit there was a faint "yes," this week not even that. She just lies there—blind, tiny, under the candlewick coverlet, the thin grey hair drawn up into a wispy knot. She has no wrinkles—the skin is tight and shiny. She appears very small—though who knows; at one time she might have been a large woman. There is no question in my mind that she was a good woman, a kind woman—responsible, although her charges as nursemaid, the seven high-spirited Murray children, must have been a handful. And who was Mr. Batchelder? Was there a Mr. Batchelder? What brought her from London to New York and into service? She was a young woman in the Boer War, a matron in World War I. The same could be said of my two grandmothers who don't seem lost in time to me. She was their contemporary. That is one thing; the process of dying at one hundred and seven another. It would seem, to observe her settling into death, a gentle process. An inarticulate murmuring goes on—an answer not to the world's queries but a commentary on what comes next. The children she cared for are lost. Whatever character I have assumed for her is lost. The interest is elsewhere. Such a delicate approach—or departure—without sound, without apprehension, no farewells. Forty years the senior of me, who am claiming to be old.

"O Father of mercies and God of all comfort, our only help in time of need, I come to Thee for help to meet the trials of advancing years." Miss Grenfell's prayer speaks to Mrs. Batchelder at her term, to me with all my old age before me. "Give me courage and patience to bear the infirmities, privations, and loneliness of old age. Help me to fight successfully its temptations to be exacting, selfish, unreasonable, irritable, and complaining. Preserve my mental faculties unimpaired to the end, keep my heart and affections warm . . . and so fit and prepare me against the hour of death that I may be able to face it fearlessly, trusting in Thy promise to be with me as I pass through the dark valley, so that departing in peace, my soul may be received into Thy everlasting Kingdom."

It was the longest prayer I had ever read to her and I was uncertain that she had heard or understood a word.

The exercise of patience, a heroic virtue in the young, is a necessity in the old who are confronted by the kingdom of heaven in an ever more explicit way. Still if we must be patient, the patient God seems the most terrifying. What does He want of us? What is He waiting for? Why does He stand there saying nothing? But Mrs. Batchelder exhibits no signs of terror.

A month and she is gone, a graveside service in the Catholic cemetery on the far side of Southampton with me and a half dozen aging, fashionable ladies, once Mrs. Batchelder's pinafored charges, listening to the last words. One sad, pretty widow. The service is brief. The late summer afternoon is clear and still.

LAST SUNDAY, ANOTHER WEDDING. Our daughter Mary Ellin married Steve Lerner, Max and Edna's middle son, as fine a wedding as the one in May, though very different. This time the ceremony took place out-of-doors on the Lerner's back lawn under a hundred-year-old pear tree halfway to the woods. Jim Morton, splendid in his vestments as cathedral dean, officiated. I gave away the bride, the second in one season. Max read from the Song of Songs and I from Ecclesiastes. The guests sat in ranks of folding chairs on the long lawn where (as Max noted in his column describing the event) deer had been grazing that morning. At the ceremony's end, under the supervision of the Hamptons' rabbi, the glass was crushed and the bride and groom were carried high in chairs among the laughing

guests. Then those who could danced the *hora.* Max grinned
with pleasure—what could be finer than to see your child
married to the child of cherished friends. Max noted further that both he and the bride's grandfather were graduates
of Ellis Island, he in 1907 and Mr. B. in 1893. Both were
Russian Jews, children of families in flight. And after over-
coming the formidable handicaps of poverty and prejudice,
both had married out of their faith, blue-eyed blondes,
which made this wedding one of interesting fractions.

Now the newlyweds have set off for Bolivia and Peru,
two dangerous places. Elizabeth Matson has returned to Los
Angeles. Katherine and Benjy, back from their wedding trip
across the States, have gone to take part in another wedding in Nashville. My book on sickness is finished and has
gone to Tim Seldes, my agent. And I am preparing to depart
for Jerusalem for three months at St. George's College to
study the Holy Land and the three great traditions whose
tangled roots are still there.

Jerusalem? Three months? Have two weddings, the specta-
cle of two new beginnings caused me to take leave of my
senses?

All summer we have had ominous news from the Middle
East. The Turks have strafed a British beach in Cyprus full
of bathing army officers and their families. "A group of
prominent rabbis" have called for the construction of a
synagogue where the Muslims' holy Dome of the Rock
presently stands. A young tourist has been shot down by
an unidentified assailant outside the wall of the Garden
Tomb. The Holy Land—a dangerous place surrounded by
dangerous places.

Some people tell me the College is a zoo where the students from the Third World don't know how to use the
facilities, with disastrous results. Others tell me the people
there don't like Jews; others say that just being in Jerusalem

is staggering, incomparable, like nothing else I'll ever experience. At any rate, I am going.

NEW YORK

A GOODBYE LUNCH WITH MY SON IRVING. He reported on the Museum Shop at MOMA where he now works, and his life in the East Village with a roommate who allows Irving to polish his college papers while he is celebrating his graduation prematurely with his multiple girlfriends.

I paid my farewell visit to Bert, now back in the nursing home, and I fear, very close to death. For a man whose bones were always near the surface, he now has no flesh on them at all. He didn't open his eyes. I tried reading aloud Max's column about Mary Ellin's and Steve's wedding. He listened for a while and then interrupted me to ask for water—the single word which he kept repeating. The rest of my visit was occupied by giving him small sips—and then "water" was replaced by "Please let me die. Please let me die." No longer a complaint, a simple whispered request. It doesn't seem possible that I shall see him again—but I have thought that before.

Later, Mary Ellin met me at a bedraggled theater downtown to see the reconstituted version of *Lost Horizon*—a movie which, although it didn't "hold up" as a theater piece, still put forth its haunting premise. I saw it first in Des Moines nearly fifty years ago. I can't remember what I, a youngster who had no idea of where he was or where he was going, thought. Perhaps I thought that it was sentimental, that it was splendid, a memorable trip, a thrilling adventure with an enviable destination.

So why am I, an old man, going to this old land, the oldest I have so far visited? Mary Ellin has any number of reasons for *not* wanting to go. Middle East precariousness—she is more susceptible than I to the multiple news reports of violence, realized or intended. She has a negligible interest in religion, any religion—her father's, her mother's, mine. She is determined to get back to the novel she has been struggling with too long, and the freelance editing which brings in much-needed money. Even though they are out of the nest, the children—newlyweds and a bachelor son—may need support, someone around.

My reasons for wanting to go are less easily defined. There is no mission I can point to. There is only my own determination to experience—not "for" experience or "for" knowledge, not to learn although that is the next closest thing—not even to search. Experience for me means to have a stretch of time that is significantly filled as it might be on retreat, or in a place where I am required to devote myself to others, such as a hospital, or an asylum or prison—that isn't to be found in my fragmentary visitations in Water Mill or Manhattan.

I went to India at least in part out of curiosity. Curiosity has nothing to do with this trip. I have some idea of what I am laying myself open to, and it has nothing to do with Sunday mornings in Des Moines with Grandpa Barrett's Gustave Dore Bible, with D. W. Griffiths or Cecil B. DeMille. I am determined to go.

NEW YORK, THREE MONTHS LATER

IT IS THE DAY AFTER CHRISTMAS and I am back in St. Luke's Hospital on the porch at Scrymser, floor seven, staring east into a roiled red and purple morning sky. Once more in that place where two years and nine months ago, March of 1984, I died and was born again: a place I had hoped never to revisit. The crevasses of Harlem are still lit in that partial way with an illuminated grid or two above a few dark towers and a flake of light—a plane rising from or drifting down into La Guardia and off to the left a sheet of grey water.

Yesterday morning I was in the hospital chapel. There on the balcony, a handful of us were weakly singing the Christmas hymns: "Hark! the Herald Angels," "Adeste Fideles," "O Little Town of Bethlehem," "Silent Night."

Then the service was over, the chaplain and organist were gone, and we waited in our hospital gowns and paper slippers for our caretakers to come and wheel or lead us away: an old lady, another old gentleman besides myself, two worn-looking younger women, and a couple in street clothes waiting for news, good or bad. Someone began to sing "The First Noel." We all joined in *a cappella*, thin and wobbly, but on key and maybe just a bit defiant. For me there was a sort of cumulative miracle, unexpected yet emphatic, a shining package with the words embedded in it.

This was the same hymn that, three months ago, I was singing in the manger at Bethlehem. There were sixteen of us, students enrolled in the long course, "The Bible and the Holy Land, Home of Three Great Faiths," at St. George's College in Jerusalem. Fifteen were hale, strong-lunged, young Third World clergymen of many denominations from many places: Taiwan, Brazil, Hong King, India, Tahiti, Cebu, Zimbabwe. And then there was me, the ringer, recently retired from the Columbia School of Journalism and push-ing seventy, and who was barely an Episcopalian. With the manger all to ourselves, and with Christmas still a season away, we sang.

Here is the sort of thing that had been going on all fall in a land where miracles were commonplace: a climb up Tabor, the Mount of Transfiguration; Masada (the funicular down, not up); up both ends of Carmel; Scopus, many times; Ein Gedi; the Herodium; a thousand steps up the Mount of Temptation (with my defective heart what was I thinking of?); up the slow slope of the Mount of the Beatitudes, looking the heart-breaking, miracle-strewn distance down over Capernaum, over Tabgha to the Sea of Galilee. Up to Belvoir, up the Mount of Olives—not, however, the seven thousand steps up Sinai, but instead looking up in awe from St. Catherine's, the site of the Burning Bush, to the red stone heap above.

Still, a lot of climbing. A pilgrim (I was after all a pilgrim) is expected to climb and visit—a lot of visits—to caves, to tunnels and tombs, to churches and palaces, tels and crypts, to Joshua's Jericho, John's Jordan, digs and open fields, Megiddo where (at the moment it seems quite likely) the final battle is to be fought, Nazareth, Cana (water into wine), Acco, Nebi Samwil, Lod, Safed, San Saaba, Gamala, Gadara (the maddened swine), Emmaus (the resurrection confirmed). The Judean wilderness, pink and mauve, spread out before me with Bethany (the raising of Lazarus), Gethsemane, the Mosque of Omar, the Temple Wall, Calvary and the Sepulcher somewhere at my back. Spots holy and not so—Sodom to the right as we rattle south past Qumran to Akaba—and everywhere a conviction of authenticity, that this is certainly where it all happened—the history, the prodigies, the miracles.

Now, the Holy Land behind me, it is as if the nurses' aide had put me in my chair with wheels, a blanket across my lap, and intentionally pushed me through all those bleak hospital corridors to a final bright eminence.

Those men in their green dusters with their masks, their bakers' hats, their knives and saws—I have survived them. It is a miracle reinforced, realized, riding on top of our thin, wispy patients' voices.

Nor is it so dire as all this obliquity would seem to suggest, to be back in the hospital, recovering, they assured me (and I don't doubt it, as they have been right before with two heart attacks and one excised cancer), from a quintuple bypass. Not dire at all, but quite homey. There was a long wait for surgery from Friday noon to early evening, the last Friday but one of Advent, and the last bypass of the week, with my wife Mary Ellin and our youngest daughter Katherine filling the time singing, not the appropriate carols, but all the songs we sang on the long drive to the beach, from the country into the city, or to Des Moines—the six of us, four children and two grownups, in our tarnished gold Chrysler station wagon with the defective shock absorbers, singing "Blue Skies," "Don't Bring Lulu," "Let's Have Another Cup of Coffee," "Mean to Me"—until they finally wheeled me away on a gurney with creaking wheels and a thin blanket up to my chin, not all that scared, a molehill being pushed to Mohammed.

Later, Mary Ellin and the three clergymen given the right to visit in the recovery room said I looked appalling, that I had as many tubes and wires hanging from me as a cuttlefish has tentacles, not a particularly pretty picture. And when they asked me how I felt, how *it* felt, I gave them all a very cold look and said, as Mary Ellin reports, "Disagreeable," answering both questions at once.

Now, for the moment, they are gone—the tubes and wires, the clergymen, my wife and daughter—and across my chest is a kind of grate, as if, were it not there, my heart might escape, swell, and flap away. Yesterday at chapel and a little later it seemed it must do just that, swell and break through. But it was contained.

My breath is shallow. I shuffle like the old man I have recently been claiming to be: not pretending now, but the real thing. Tubeless and wireless, I look in my lavatory mirror, and the face is grey almost as death—but death departing, not homing in.

Sometime during the eleven weeks I was in Israel, Mary Ellin had her sixtieth birthday. Katherine and Benjy gave the party, their first in their new apartment on Washington Heights, and read my greetings from the Holy Land. I celebrated our thirty-fifth anniversary in a sleeping bag on the cooling sands of the Sinai. And when I was back in Jerusalem, Mary Ellin phoned to tell me that Elizabeth, our eldest, was expecting a baby, our first grandchild, next May.

Coming up from walking Molly in Riverside Park, I had felt a little odd, short of breath, slightly dizzy: not much to go on, a ghost of older symptoms. After climbing every mountain in the Holy Land, to succumb to a few steps up from Riverside Drive to Claremont Avenue, which was what I was doing, seemed ludicrous.

So I am back where I have been many times before. They have, I am told, split me open like a chicken, rearranged things, and sewed me back up, as good as new, or at least a lot better than I was.

Mary Ellin reports that her father called, asking, before she could tell him the latest development, to talk to me. He had just got the card I sent him from Jerusalem, and with that curiosity which at ninety-eight is still not satisfied, demanded an accounting of what was going on in the land of his forefathers. Mary Ellin gave him my current address. "Oh, my God," he said, which was, in my opinion, an appropriate response. The in-laws' flowers are conspicuous on my hospital windowsill along with a handmade Christmas card from our artist son, and the animals from the Christmas stocking our middle daughter put together for me: a *papier-mâché* zebra, a glass frog, a stuffed seal. Beyond the pane, past the largest Gothic church in Christendom, a mountain in grey stone, are the pigeons, the peacocks, and the chickens, in the sun of the cathedral yard.

. . .

Temper the wind to the shorn lamb—where do the old enter into that prescription? Are the old shorn, or are they covered by the wool of experience? Are the bright-eyed and bushy-tailed young (certainly not a shorn image) the truly shorn, having not yet grown their winter coats? It is another of those sayings that flips under examination, and then flips again. Did this latest sickness, did my sojourn in the Holy Land, shear me or furnish me with another, thicker blanket? And is it more desirable, after all, to be shorn—better to be exposed than protected?

Indeed, at sixty-six, should I have been camping out in the Sinai, in the sand in a sleeping bag, celebrating a distant anniversary with questionable food and drink? Should I have been staring sleepless across a dry, stony valley to a soaring cliff that could be, under an almost full moon, a sleeping city, a deserted monastery, a derelict temple? Should I have strayed so far from the Holy Land as Wadi Natrum, across the Red Sea, across the Nile? I staggered from monastery to monastery, real ones now, no hallucinations. Across the Libyan Desert, a grim stretch of it where the Desert Fathers once sat in front of their caves weaving baskets, eating dates and unleavened bread, welcoming the occasional seeking stranger, growing old staring into the wavering distance, and me disoriented by a bilious stomach and a defective inner ear, trailing a group of hearty tourists from the Netherlands who got there first.

As the group elder, I had been allowed to carry the cross into the Church of the Holy Sepulcher and read the meditation before the tomb. I had been the first to read the Scripture and designate the hymns to be sung in the red wastes of the Sinai alongside the beehive huts—"the tombs of the damned." "A jolly desert," Lawrence of Arabia told Robert Graves. The Jews thought otherwise.

At St. George's College, I was not only the oldest but

also the only unordained student. But no one among that group of young clergymen was likely to take back to their congregations on five continents more than I, speechless, took to an unwitting congregation on that chapel balcony at St. Luke's Hospital. And it seemed to me a fair and appropriate distribution.

The list for my last day in Jerusalem:
>   The Dome of the Rock
>   The Fountain of Sultan Qa'it Bay
>   St. Anne's
>   The Marmaluke Houses
>   The Abyssinian Chapel
>   The Church of St. Mary Magdalene
>   The Tomb of the Kings
>   The Bethesda Pool

I got as far as the Damascus Gate, where I met a classmate, a worldly Australian destined for a lifetime in a monastery in England, who said that four Arab students had been shot by Israeli soldiers up north and the army was pouring into the Old City by the Dung Gate in expectation of bad trouble. I turned back.

In the Holy Land everyone has fertile ground for anger. The old. The young. The Jews. The Arabs. When I heard the grievances of the Jews, I felt sorry for the Arabs. When I heard the Arabs, it was the Jews I felt sorry for. Facing the young, I did not know what to think.

So approaching three score and ten I have managed a peak experience. Does a pilgrimage to Jerusalem and back make me a little short of being old? Pilgrims are of no particular age. But perhaps pilgrims who come back are not yet quite old. And now with my quintuple bypass I am back yet again.

1987

*1987*___

SICKNESS IS A VALLEY that one climbs out of: a ravine with a beginning, a middle, and an end but no horizons. It is a deep shadow as the psalmist says, with no attributable source of light, or just a flicker, if there seems to be any light at all.

Old age, I would say, is a plain, an *alto plano*, with nothing when you come out onto it but horizon; there are few discernible features, at least at first glance, no tracks to follow. Accustomed to limits, to guidelines, to markers, you stand there stunned, amazed. You haven't had such a sense of space since you were twenty—the splendor, the terror of it. All that out there ahead of you is to be explored, to be prospected, mapped, traversed. And then came World War II, and the space was filled. It had been before, I suppose, but with ghosts, mirages cast forward from the past. After that nothing was really empty.

Now the space seems clear again and it is up to me to fill it, to make sense of it. Sickness will not help me. Sickness from here on out will have a new and less compelling meaning—sickness for the old is more a commentary than a challenge.

If my memory serves me, my fear of my parents' death when I was young was much greater than that for my own death now that I am old. For all my mortal illnesses, for all death's nearness, it remains a matter of remote speculation. The death of contemporaries does not convince me of my own mortality—quite the opposite. The death of parents, however does—the memory of their deaths—the fact of their deaths and of grandparents gone before them. Their going has nothing to do with my cleverness in surviving. It is a prophecy of things to come.

The last quarter of life—why not call it that rather than old age?—has no defined beginning, no certain end: It is one's lifetime, whatever the total turns out to be, divided by four. Those left behind can do the arithmetic.

WASHINGTON, D.C.

FOR THE FIRST TIME we are visiting in one of our children's houses—actually spending the night, some sort of landmark. The house—Mary Ellin and Steve's—stands on a side street off 16th, a street lined by trees, a row of small nineteenth-century brick dwellings in different colors, with stoops and small back yards. Something about the street and house reminds us of Greenwich Village, West 11th Street, where we lived when the children were small. Inside it is warm and book-lined, furnished with family hand-me-downs, wedding presents, a dining room table from us, a Lerner rug, an old upright piano, treasures from Steve's globe-trotting days, a Hindu carving from a temple cart, a Mexican *santo* by the living room fireplace, Hans Namuth's color photograph of Andy Warhol, poster size, in the downstairs bathroom. Two cats: Nelson and Winnie.

In the morning we drove out to Nora and Farwell Smith's farm on a high hill in Maryland overlooking the Pool of the

Potomac—a house rented from Paul Nitze who has a two thousand acre spread on the banks of the river across from Virginia—a vast view. The Judaean Wilderness with water and trees.

Mr. Nitze came for lunch. Recently turned eighty, he has spent the last several years in intense activity representing the United States in its negotiations with Russia. The lunchtime conversation had to do with that, with Gorbachev's latest speech. Nitze also brought up his association nearly fifty years ago with Henry Wallace and how mistaken was the popular view of H.W. as soft and bubbleheaded—the view shared by most, but not all, of my Iowa relatives. Cousin Ed, who worked for him, saw him somewhat differently. Like Ed, Nitze found Wallace sharp to a fault, crafty even, and anything but muddled. A bleeding-heart liberal who makes a fortune in middle age and keeps adding to it is not muddled nor bubbleheaded. The bubble has long since burst.

Nitze is preparing to go into the latest negotiations with the Soviet Union, playing, one suspects, a crucial role. Certainly there is no indication of dilapidation about him. To see such a man at eighty was instructive.

Nitze's wife, an accomplished horsewoman, had recently died a slow and agonizing death of emphysema. At the end, coming out of her coma, she suddenly said in a clear, firm voice, "I have made the jump. I have made the jump." Then an hour or two later she asked, "Can I open the gate?" whereupon she died.

CLAREMONT AVENUE

COMING BACK FROM THE WEEKEND Mary Ellin expresses a desire to start all over again, or at least go back twenty-five or thirty years. I shush her, although I too feel quite often the pull of those early years, not so much to live them over—since I know that intellectually to be a fatuous, if not a wicked hankering—but the pull of a shared, selective remembrance. Our first small house and garden with its spectacular view that we, the honeymooners, rented in Sicily, our first Christmas, the first holiday dinner cooked and served to our amazed parents, the first baby—there before we had a chance to catch our breath and settle down —and the next and the next, and the last. Our first real house bought and mortgaged—a long time in coming. The childrens' first day at school. There was the excitement of the first byline, the first book. An appreciation of those years when I was living them was only dimly felt through the distractions of the present and the future, of earning a living, a reputation, of making mistakes and correcting them.

As for the fatuity of hankering after the past: Would it have been good to go back to grammar school, as I often thought wistfully from unhappy junior high? Or to repeat those golden years in junior high as seen from the disruptions of high school? College for the moment seemed a fair balance, just about right, but even then there were flickers of discontent, comparisons in favor of what had gone before. As for what came next . . .

And what about the kind of starting over that involves multiple marriages, multiple affairs, multiple jobs, where the same mistaken expectations are disappointed again and again. It is better in most cases to persist in difficulties and see what comes next than to extricate oneself and then duplicate the problems up to the same sticking point. It is better to keep moving slowly, steadily, no sticking, no balking, no clinging repetitions, straight on, or crooked on—but still *on*, step by step, revelation by revelation, about oneself, about everything. Over the fence. Through the gate.

Or to put it another way. As you grow older the fantasy of doing it all over again becomes progressively less attractive. Past performance gives no guarantee that the mistakes you made would not be even worse the next time round, or that yesterdays' errors wouldn't grow dreary with repetition. It is like the realization that to change places with anyone is not worth considering, that we have no idea of what is going on over there where the turf seems so much greener. "If the young knew; if the old could." They don't, they can't. They never will. They shouldn't.

Another bedtime conversation: "Men are what they are, women are what they think they are," I say. At first glance it seemed an interesting idea. It became more interesting when I considered the exact opposite could be affirmed: Women are what they are, men what they think they are. That may be the truer of the two statements. Then why did the other occur to me first? "Because you are a man," says Mary Ellin. Perhaps it's because I assume being is more important than thinking. Because thinking has to do with art, or creativity, or sensitivity; and being with religion, a religion that doesn't tolerate distance or objectivity. Which brings one to consider men and women vis a vis age. There must be a difference. Or must there? Why cannot a convergence in the old that obliterates the difference be yet another advantage of old age—an opportunity to understand the other half of the human race—to think and be at the same time?

ENCOURAGED BY THE LIMITATIONS of yet another convalescence I am sifting through the poets of the last century who seemed more optimistic about old age than today's. Corny perhaps in the first reading until you get there yourself. At the top of the list:

> *Grow old along with me!*
> *The best is yet to be,*

The last of life, for which the first was made:
Our times are in His hand
Who saith "A whole I planned,
"Youth shows but half; trust God; see all
   nor be afraid."

Robert Browning wrote "Rabbi Ben Ezra" when he was not yet fifty. He had thirty more years to correct his mistake if indeed he felt he had made one.

Not at all. At seventy-seven in the last stanza of the epilogue to *Asolanda,* his last book, he wrote:

No, at noon-day in the battle of man's worktime
Greet the unseen with a cheer!
Bid him forward, breast and back
As either should be.
"Strive and thrive!" cry "Speed—fight on, fare ever
There as here!"

Thomas Hardy, the old unbeliever who had asked that "Rabbi Ben Ezra" be read to him more than once in the weeks before his death, already had written in "An Ancient to Ancients" a telling statement on the subject. The last four stanzas are worth quoting:

We who met sunrise sanguine-souled,
   Gentlemen,
Are wearing weary. We are old;
These younger press; we feel our rout
Is imminent to Aïdes' den—
That evening shades are stretching out,
   Gentlemen!

And yet, though ours be failing frames,
   Gentlemen,
So were some others' history names

Who trode their track light-limbed and fast
As these youth, and not alien
From enterprise, to their long last,
   Gentlemen,

Sophocles, Plato, Socrates,
   Gentlemen,
Pythagoras, Thucydides,
Herodotus and Homer,—yea,
Clement, Augustin, Origen,
Burnt brightlier towards their setting-day,
   Gentlemen,

And ye, red-lipped and smooth-browed; list
   Gentlemen,
Much is there waits you we have missed;
Much lore we leave you worth the knowing,
Much, much has lain outside our ken:
Nay, rush not: time serves: we are going,
   Gentlemen.

There is a particularly charming vignette of the ancient Hardy in Robert Graves' *Goodbye to All That*. After four grueling years of World War I, minutely and painfully described, Graves tells of himself and his young wife on a cross-country bicycle tour from Oxford, paying Hardy a visit at his house in Dorchester. There is nothing to pity in this old fellow who is a bit quirky, perhaps, but ultimately straight on. No surprise, then, that such a man could write such a poem. Thomas Hardy told the young couple to come back whenever they felt like it, but however they may have felt, they never found in their busy young lives the time.

But of all poets perhaps the most eloquent on old age is Tennyson, Hardy's near contemporary—they shared fifty years of the nineteenth century. Tennyson, the author of "Ulysses" and "Tithonus," not only wrote of old age, he himself was a paradigm for old age in the midst of the damaging confusions of those years.

At seventy-two, he published "Despair."

> *Hoped for a dawn, and it came, but the promise*
> *had faded away;*
> *We had past from a cheerless night to the glare*
> *of a drearier day;*
> *He is only a cloud and a smoke who was once a*
> *pillar of fire,*
> *The guess of a worm in the dust and a shadow*
> *of its desire—*

One could hardly sink lower, and yet four years later came "The Ancient Sage."

> *Await the last and largest sense to make*
> *The phantom walls of this illusion fade,*
> *And shew us that the world is wholly fair.*

As he grew old and frail himself, Tennyson told a friend inquiring after his condition, "I cannot help being troubled by the terrible excitement of spring."

At eighty-one, he had this question to ask in "By an Evolutionist":

> *What hast thou done for me, grim Old Age, save*
> *breaking my bones on the rack?*
> *Would I had past in the morning that looked so*
> *bright from afar . . .*

His answer:

> *Done for thee? starved the wild beast that was*
> *linked with thee eighty years back.*

> *Less weight now for the ladder of heaven that*
> *hangs on a star . . .*

The next year, recently recovered from a desperate illness, he wrote in a twenty-minute crossing on the ferry
from Lymington to Yarmouth, the poem his son Hallam
called "the crown of your life's work" and one that even a
hundred years later must give any aging person salutary
pause, if not a thrill of amazement, at the old man's nerve:

> *Sunset and evening star,*
> *And one clear call for me!*
> *And may there be no moaning of the bar,*
> *When I put out to sea,*
>
> *But such a tide as moving seems asleep,*
> *Too full for sound and foam*
> *When that which drew from out the boundless deep*
> *Turns again home.*

Has bathos ever been so confidently approached and yet
been so successfully skirted? Tennyson's is a vision I had in
my skeptical middle years forbidden myself. But now its
conviction grows.

WATER MILL

YESTERDAY ANOTHER BIRTHDAY, my sixty-seventh. It
started in a drizzle and ended pale blue and clear. I went to
ten o'clock service, bought and planted a dozen marigolds
(whose blossoms the rabbits have already nibbled away),
shopped for the birthday dinner Mary Ellin cooked for me,
and visited Augusta, one of the nursing home ladies. She

has had a stroke and is now lying in the old folks' wing at the hospital with a tube up her nose and another in her veins; her eyes open but not in touch with anything outside herself.

It is the second day of the Iran-Contra hearings and of Gary Hart's self-inflicted ordeal. All the children called.

Erik Erikson says, "Healthy children will not fear life if their parents have integrity enough not to fear death." Our children's fearlessness is a responsibility we have to acknowledge. I am under the impression that for the time being, thanks to the episode in St. Luke's three years ago, I am free of the fear of death.

Irving has done a large collage, if that is an adequate description, nine painstakingly detailed lunettes of me being sick, getting well. This collage is a remarkable object made from a thousand small pieces of paper adding up to me convalescent—like a series of small paintings, but not paintings, paper intarsia. Not flattering but he got the right idea. He is a very clever young fellow.

Today in the mail arrived from my agent Tim Seldes, not a late birthday present, but the manuscript of the sickness book I have been working on for the past two years. His letter tells me that no matter how charming it may be to friends and family, or if not charming at least morbidly interesting, he has reluctantly decided after getting two rejections that to submit it elsewhere would be futile. So there it sits in its bundle waiting to be put in some lower drawer. Except, in a gesture of defiance, I have sent the manuscript off to Alan Williams, an old friend and the first editor of my youth, and a copy of the last chapter to Willy Knapp, an even older friend at the *New Yorker.*

. . .

Now we are waiting for the phone call to tell us Elizabeth
has had her baby.

—ɯ—

PETER BARRETT MATSON, ten pounds eight ounces,
arrived May 15, the exact day we were told to expect him
many months ago. He came onto the scene in the hour after
his great-grandfather had been chosen "person of the week"
by ABC News and eulogized by Ted Koppel on the occasion
of his ninety-ninth birthday four days earlier. That sets
Peter, the first of the new generation, firmly in the center
of the May babies; me and Mr. B. on one side, Irving and
Eddie on the other, a masculine month.

The excitement of the phone call announcing Peter's
arrival completely obliterated my consideration of the
solemn fact that this, according to the Hindus, is not only
a birthday, a day of family rejoicing, but the first day of my
old age, the *real* first day, the beginning of the most important stage of my life on earth. Some time after the lights
were finally out—through the residual excitement and the
surrounding darkness—came the realization, not only that
Peter was here, but that whether I wanted it or not, I had
been promoted. As for Mary Ellin, I guess she has been promoted as well, whatever her age or appearance. She
certainly doesn't act or look the part.

SANTA MONICA

BABY PETER AT FIVE DAYS appears in much better shape
than recent arrivals usually are, certainly than his jet-lagged
grandparents. A big, good-looking boy, blonde, blue-eyed,

he is satisfied with himself and his surroundings—glad, it would seem, to be here. Lying in his bassinet in Elizabeth and Sasha's rented bungalow he is the still center of the confusion attending an imminent move, evidenced by half-packed boxes of books, of china, emptied closets and cupboards.

The boy, the symbol, lies there on his stomach in a blue bunting, or in his yellow Dr. Dentons—whether his eyes are closed or open, he is not communicating in any usual way—still he is very much a fact, assimilating his own arrival in some interior, integral fashion. From where? And bound for where? An air of interest, of surprise even. We grown-ups are very busy. He, the reason for it all, isn't in the least. Lily the cat, a blue-grey, longhaired object of beauty, sits quietly observing. Not really quiet at all, she is waiting—she has attacked me once for an intrusive finger and is ready to strike again.

So far in all this bustle there is no particular sensation of newness or strangeness to mark this new and strange stage in all our lives. Peter is the preeminent fact.

The boy is here and a week ago he wasn't. That is what is remarkable. And, of course, he has all those qualities—endearing, pathetic, intimidating—that an infant possesses. He is holdable, serviceable, and apparently encompassable until one begins to think of all the questions that are wrapped up in that one small bundle.

So I sit on the white-webbed plastic swing in the back yard reading. I hang up the laundry—take it down—there is no dryer in Elizabeth's temporary home. I go to the supermarket and run errands in our rented Pontiac, pack a few records and books while Mary Ellin cooks and washes up and makes herself more substantially useful.

At night we return to our 1920s Spanish Colonial hotel, occupied, it would seem, only by us and the bright white-haired lady manageress with a colored photograph of

Ronald Reagan on the wall of her crowded cubicle. And either in the morning before we start out or in the evening when we return, we read the *Los Angeles Times* and the *New York Times* filled with the latest indecencies of Irangate and Wall Street.

And so the boy, the first grandchild, enters his second week.

—॥॥—

HANGING OUT THE WASH, as I am the oldest and weakest member of the party, is my assignment. In Des Moines in the '20s and '30s it was the youngest's chore. At Trabuco, the commune of my young manhood, once a fortnight it was my duty to carry the sheets and towels out to the line stretched at the upper margin of the phenomenal view—to be bleached by the sun, impregnated by the odor of lemon and sage, and gathered in before the bell for evening prayers. In Jerusalem, nine months ago, I was hanging my laundry out on the flat roof of St. George's College, look-ing out over the old city and on to the Mount of Olives with Bethany beyond—all that out there past my damp under-wear and socks. Clotheslines and pins stretching from earliest memory to now, a lifetime of hanging out the wash, taking it down, putting it away to be soiled and washed and hung out another day.

I test it. It is still damp. I go back to my magazine arti-cle on old age and am confronted by Lewis Carroll:

> "You are old, Father William," the young man said,
> "And your hair has become very white;
> "And yet you incessantly stand on your head—
> "Do you think, at your age, it is right?"
>
> "In my youth," Father William replied to his son,
> "I feared it might injure my brain;

"But now that I'm perfectly sure I have none,
"Why, I do it again and again."

Next comes King Lear in his bereaved dotage saying to Cordelia:

We two alone will sing like birds i' th' cage;
When thou dost ask me blessing, I'll kneel down
And ask of thee forgiveness. So we'll live
And pray, and sing, and tell old tales, and laugh
At gilded butterflies . . .

Should I kneel down and ask forgiveness of Peter? Why indeed not? What better time or person or place? Has the world been improved at all from my being in it? What have we old ones left as our heritage to the young? What when they are old will be their legacy? One hopes better than ours, but history, as we are capable of understanding it, says probably no chance. Still, hope is constant and is the answer to all apparent defeats. And it is the exact same hope for Peter and his parents, for us, and the generation before us. Hope standing us on our head. Hope asking each others' forgiveness.

So Elizabeth, our oldest, is now a mother, as Mary Ellin, the oldest, once presented her own parents with their first grandchild, the female equivalent of Peter—blonde, blue-eyed, chirping in the alcove off our bedroom in my bachelor apartment, the Madison Avenue bus gasping as it climbed toward 72nd Street below our front windows.

—ɯ—

YESTERDAY I WENT TO VISIT UNCLE BILL, at eighty-eight the oldest Barrett, as Peter is the youngest. He lives by himself in a bungalow in Van Nuys, in a long narrow pale green house with a gallery and, running the length of it, a garden, mostly clipped hedges and rose bushes, with a square concrete patio. Inside the house the principal piece of furniture is a grand piano painted a pinkish white. With it in the living room stands the refrigerator, almost as large, moved in for convenience's sake although there seem to be two kitchens. The house is at the end of a *cul de sac* and for some reason, the gallery where we sat and talked was cooler than all the rest of the San Fernando Valley which was very hot indeed.

White-haired and clear-eyed, Bill looks fit and is carefully groomed, in a canary-yellow sweater, white shirt and slacks. He attributes his mental and physical condition to my Aunt Gladys (long deceased), God, and a devoted daughter (my cousin Elizabeth), in that order. Gladys, his second wife (his first, Sara, stayed on in Des Moines to care for my grandfather) moved Bill to Southern California fifty years ago and saw that he took care of himself, although I witnessed the two of them eat a quart of ice cream at a sitting.

This Bill, then is Poppa's naughty younger brother whom I remember with his glistening accordion and patent leather hair. The pink piano is the accordion's final replacement, a symbol of the prosperity, good health, and regular habits which came with California and Aunt Gladys. There is a handsome black cat to be patted before I leave and a short tinkling refrain on the seldom-played piano (the little girl next door to whom it will be left sometimes comes in to practice). A tribute to my father-in-law is Bill's intention. *Bill Barrett's Cardinals* played all the great songs back then, waltzes and foxtrots and novelties: "What'll I Do?" "Remember," "All Alone," "Putting on the Ritz," "Everybody's Doing It." "Remember"—that's the one he now tinkles, leaning away from the keys, eyes closed.

TRABUCO

CONFUCIUS SAYS, "The wise take pleasure in water, but the benevolent in mountains; because wisdom moves about, but benevolence remains still. Wisdom leads to happiness: benevolence to a long life."

That our first grandchild has chosen Southern California to be born in with its mountains next to the sea has, for Mary Ellin and me, a particular resonance. Wisdom and old age may be fighting a rear guard action hereabouts, or perhaps just re-forming for the next assault, but Confucius' mountains and sea are certainly here in striking juxtaposition. In our respective youths they struck both Mary Ellin and myself, born elsewhere and faraway, as the anteroom to paradise.

Now on the freeway to Santa Ana and beyond, the entire landscape toward the mountains, toward the sea, is unrecognizable. Lot by bulldozed lot, grove by fallen grove, the approach to Paradise has become nightmare alley, six lanes wide, aimed through the wreckage of God's country at Tijuana.

I am on my way to Trabuco, to the left, into the foothills going south. While the Matsons move to their new house in Mar Vista, I have been given leave, in fact encouraged, to take this trip to the ranch Gerald Heard hoped to establish as a spiritual outpost, the Southern California equivalent of Bede Griffiths' ashram in Tamil Nadu, a bridge between East and West, the old and new, science and religion. Today it is a Vedanta monastery. The resident monks have allowed me to make a weekend's return.

Leaving the highway I climb into a limbo of dun-colored houses planted where groves of oranges and avocados used to be and finally enter a canyon that looks vaguely familiar, with mesquite, sycamore, and live oak lining a dry stream bed. There is a brand-new gate—left open, a recently surfaced road up the hill. At the top, almost as I remember it, is Gerald's ranch—the workshops, the pumphouse and garage, the dormitory under the big shuddering pepper tree, the main house with its belfry and seventeenth-century bell. The brick and stucco walls descend in stages through the cloisters toward the octagonal oratory, all at first glance unchanged, exactly as Gerald conceived it, and Felix Greene, his builder and "prior," executed it—a minor miracle in a rationed world at war. The surrounding landscape, however, is transformed. A man-made lake sits below the saddle where once there was a valley of uninterrupted green. On the hill high above the dormitory, once a naked silhouette, is a white New England church and next to it a fussy ranch house with suburban plantings. The brown slope on the far side of the ravine is scarred with a ploughed S, a precaution against catastrophic fire. On three sides the world has taken over. Only the mountains to the east, purple and tall, stand as they did.

Closer in, I see that the olives around the oratory and below the cloisters have grown from the twigs that we stuck into the ground into mature trees. There are still a half dozen lemons standing in the grove that was dying from lack of water when I left forty years ago. Through this same grove I had fled, past the prickly pear into the live oaks, with Aldous Huxley in pursuit—poor blind fellow, he didn't stand a chance. Gerald, no doubt, had set him on me in the hope he might help me recapture a little of my dying enthusiasm for the celibate life. A short inspirational talk should do the trick. No such luck—a fortnight later I was on the train back to Iowa and all that came after.

Now on the far side of the still-struggling lemons is a well-kept garden—fenced, with a small lath house beside it. In the garden are huge clumps of chard, their branches wide as palm leaves, beans, squash, a row of berries under black plastic, marigolds for the altar in the oratory. Beyond —a busy pump.

What does all this mean to me, a new grandfather? What is the same, what is different? When I lived here I was just twenty-six, fresh, maybe slightly bedraggled, from four years in the service, two of them on tropical islands off the equator. In 1946 there was no human habitation in sight. We had it all to ourselves—the uninterrupted view to the sea, the mountains behind which symbolized the uncluttered life I intended henceforth to lead. We were young, the dozen or so committed ones intent upon changing the world for the better. We were the shock troops for a new dispensation, "a new morality." I can still hear Gerald quoting Archbishop Temple: "The right relation between Prayer and Conduct is not that Conduct is supremely important and Prayer may help it; but that Prayer is supremely important and Conduct tests it."

The current residents, eight Vedanta monks in their fifties or a little beyond, with at least one life behind them, are perhaps holding their own. Those hopeful ones who had been here with me are scattered or dead, most of them before they could be labeled "truly old." Betsy and Felix, Edwin and Lucille, Etta Jean, Miriam, two Rays, and a David, of them all, perhaps only I, the acknowledged old man, remember exactly what we were up to. I have never forgotten.

In my room I listen to Gerald on old age, passages recorded when he still had many troubling years to go. His voice is in the words—that emphatic voice with just the right amount of breath and tonsils, of spittle and phlegm. As always he is prophetic—uncannily so: "It will certainly

require a revolution—in the literal sense of the word—
a revolution in our whole outlook, if we are to get this
matter of old age straight. But if we don't not only shall we
have an increasing number of elderlies on our hands,
creatures alive, but, like Saul on Gilboa, repenting that their
life is still whole in them, a pest and bore to themselves and
to all around them, but we shall have a society gravely
handicapped by this sagging load at its upper end. We shall
have a generation of senescents, costly to keep, useless for
production and, final frustration, utterly unlovely and
unloveable. . . . When we examine it we see that the problem of old age, is only that extreme point—like gangrene
in the foot—where the sick state of the whole age . . .
becomes first evident."

The dire warning followed by the good news, the
answer—a typical Gerald ploy: "It may be, as hygiene and
discipline of diet gain on us, we may recover the extensive
period of healthy old age that seems to belong to people
who have lived according to tradition. If that is so we may
yet see, if we will only make our spiritual knowledge equal
to our physiological, a recovered old age when many may
go far toward freedom for themselves and to becoming real
inspirations to the age groups below them."

There you have Gerald *in petto*, brindle beard wagging,
chalk in hand, in the cloister if the weather is fine, if not,
in the refectory in front of a blazing fire of eucalyptus logs
telling it like it was . . . and is . . . and will be. The threat
of hell first—the promise of a heaven to come. The trial,
then, in the nick of time, the reward. Like life if you choose
to live it front to back.

Bad news at lunch. One of the monks back from an errand
into town says the hills to the west and down the valley
will be filled with condominiums if the developers don't get

the necessary financing for a baseball stadium and adjacent parking lot.

The struggle goes on for these aging men of good will gathered around the long steel-topped table as it did for us youngsters, who came out of the horror of war. The trick is to try to live in a world where the clutter, the noise are closing in and the only space, the only peace that has a chance is that diminishing plot inside us. But wasn't it always so? We were right then; they are right now. Everyone is just a little older, a little wearier.

If I define my purpose in life as "to understand," is there any moment then that this purpose need be abandoned, that to understand can be recognized as untenable? I would say not. It is something that can be persisted in to the end—never quite achieved, always worth trying for. Like love. To understand, to love, such ends consume one's means forever.

So in my mind I juxtapose a ranch in the California foothills alongside a small house in Mar Vista, my youth and my old age.

The new family is in their new house. A room for Peter, a room for Elizabeth and Sasha, and in the back a narrow bed for a single visitor or maybe two young, passionate ones. The furniture and pictures look just right in the sunny white stucco living room that stretches across the front of the house: The colors are a restful green, a dusty blue. The backyard with its giant avocado and cypress promises a pleasant garden. The garage will be Sasha's studio. When Peter fusses (he has developed a slight colic) they put him on their new clothes dryer which hums and jiggles as though it had always been there to calm him.

No more hanging out the wash.

NEW YORK AND WATER MILL

BACK FROM THE WEST COAST, as we came into the apartment from the airport our phone was ringing. It was Willy Knapp telling me that the *New Yorker* wanted my piece. I'll be hearing from an editor shortly. A week later Alan Williams offered me a substantial advance for the privilege of publishing my unpublishable book. There was little or no editing to be done, he told me; it just needs a new title.

A few weeks after that, sitting on our back lawn, Alan has an idea. *Spare Days,* taken from the Herbert poem about gratitude, is his choice for a title. Now I can't even remember what my alternate was.

—м—

IT IS LATE SEPTEMBER and Elizabeth and Sasha have brought Peter back to New York to be baptized. None of our babies were baptized. When they were infants Mary Ellin and I were churchless. There were rumors that Mrs. B., a devout Catholic retread, had seen to it baby by baby— citizens' baptisms. Elizabeth at thirteen took it upon herself to be baptized and confirmed by the bishop in the same cathedral where Peter was now scheduled to be officially blessed and where I am a regular communicant.

By the time I began going to church again the children were teenagers and not particularly interested, although they were fascinated by St. Clements, the church I chose for my reentry into the Christian community. The sanctuary at St. Clements did double duty as an avant garde theater so that we worshipped in sets left over from the Saturday night performances, ladders and spare tires from Arabel, a cage and a few palm fronds from *Pinksville,* a bleak Illinois kitchen from *Sexual Perversity in Chicago.* There were great doings on Epiphany and Palm Sunday as well as Christmas and Easter. The first baptism Katherine, aged eleven, witnessed had a devout young man and woman in a tin tub nude and, if my memory serves me, armed with water pistols aimed at the congregation. The service, like Great-grandmother Helen's death, was written up in *Time*. That was the early Seventies. We are now in the late Eighties. Who knows quite what the children believe? Mary Ellin remains a hold-out—her mother's iron-clad Catholicism, her father's secular Jewishness canceling each other out.

Peter's ceremony is held in the cathedral baptistry, a handsome octagonal chamber which doubles as a columbarium. A small group of friends and relatives gather around the font where Henry Sturtevant (once pastor of St. Clements, now a groom at Belmont Racetrack), along with our friend Jim Morton, the cathedral dean, officiate as they have at last year's weddings. Peter, splendid in a christening dress twice his length, awaits the event on a padded bench along the baptistry wall, caught in a memorable photograph in which he seems to be blissfully levitating.

—⚉—

WITH THE COLD WEATHER my Meunieres syndrome has returned—my oldest resident complaint except for the ocular migraine and the sharp sweet ache in my upper arm left over from junior high. One would think that my accommodation of afflictions more severe might have moderated these lesser ones. But no, in St. Saviours, three chapels beyond the one where Peter was baptized, having just read the Old Testament lesson, a bleak passage from Ezra, I am suddenly unable to stand, let alone kneel, and am carted home by faithful friends more alarmed than I. Is this Meunieres or a stroke? In another fit since then, the world wobbles, careens. As many times before, I write to pin it down.

I write, and slowly it disappears, like all my afflictions great and small. It slowly fades away until the next time. The jottings are random:

❧ When you are young you see God as father, teacher, boss, master, healer, collaborator, adversary, and—if you have the vocation—lover. For the old He is judge-forgiver (those two always go together), and lover for sure. The rest of God's roles fall away. In youth we fight our way to God in whatever guise He appears. In old age there is a back door, a service entrance—an easy way. The prayers of the young are arduous—of the old, gentle.

But these are all ideas and God is not an idea—He is reality—and the ideas are simply pops and flashes that dimly illuminate or distract us from reality.

St. Paul said it better, but then it bears resaying.

❧ With the years the need for comparison with others fades away—comparing who is smartest, who is prettiest, strongest, most talented—in the spelling bee, football field, ballroom, musical-chairs vision of life. We come to realize that smart, pretty, strong, talented or not, we are unique. No one is quite like us, whatever we are. And at the same time there is the growing conviction, the experience of communion and sympathy with more and more of our fellow creatures. Envy is unsustainable on at least these two counts, and the constant need to compare and criticize dwindles away.

❧ Would I prefer to know the old or the young Michelangelo, Verdi, Beethoven, Tolstoy, Titian, St. John, Siddhartha, Confucius? That is a cruel question but upon consideration the obvious answer is perhaps not so obvious.

❧ It is a fact of everyone's old age that no one has achieved all that he or she set out to do—that even to the most apparently successful there is only partial satisfaction and to the least aspiring the same. If, as one might assume, lack of satisfaction and achievement is the universal condition, what indeed does that empty space represent? Not a defeat, I am convinced—it is a prompting to change at the latest possible date one's aspiration to something where partial achievement is complete satisfaction, where even the choice and will is justification.

❧"When the evening of this life comes," said St. John of the Cross, "you will be judged on love." His is a compelling directive to the old. Cumulative love, some might assume, is the sum total of one's good and loving deeds throughout life. I see it as one's ability to love right now at the end of life. A spiritual temperature—a fever of love—is perhaps an indication of a lifetime's regimen or hygiene—but it may also be a sudden infection, a carrying away, in which the prodigal son—doddering and grey-haired, shivering and hot with the emotion that has possessed him—returns.

❧ The habit of cheerfulness is invaluable to the old. Like any habit it has its moments of inconvenience, of inappropriateness. "Why," the burdened ones ask, with a disapproving frown, "is the old fool always so goddamned cheerful? There is nothing to be cheerful about." Come to think of it, there never is. Thinking too much in the wrong direction or in any direction away from where we are will make us glum. So stay put on top of the glumness or sink through it. Be content to be labeled a cheerful fool who I warrant will be revisited sooner, if visitation is what you wish, than the glum naysayer.

There—I have written myself out of it.

—⚘—

TODAY IS DECEMBER FIRST, Aunt Helene's birthday. A cold day in Iowa when she was born, the second of my Kruidenier grandparents' six children. Cold or not she lasted longest of the six—by a margin of fifteen years, twenty-five in my mother's case. She was ninety-three when she died.

What was her secret? No cigarettes, no liquor? When we were young, spending a winter in California with Grandmother Kruidenier, Aunt Helene's breakfast was what she called her "health cocktail," half olive oil, half orange juice on which she floated a raw egg. We watched her goggle-eyed while she downed it without gagging in one long, steady draught.

Each morning while the rest of us were still in bed, she did her Swedish calisthenics and put aside a regular hour for devotional reading, New Thought, and Unity—truth in leaflets and small, paper-bound books. She would invite her nephews and nieces in to share a bit of the packaged wisdom, apparently to no avail. She could wait.

She had met her future husband, a traveling man, on a bench in Balboa Park in San Diego where she was inviting the spirit. She married him a few days later and returned home permanently after her wedding night, or maybe during it. To my knowledge she never saw Arthur Converse again although she kept his name for the rest of her life. The name without the game. Maybe that was what explained her longevity. More likely it was the fact that she was small and trim, the smallest of the three sisters and three brothers and the only one with red hair.

Or maybe it was just her ability to stand still, growing smaller, frailer, whiter, waiting for me, her nephew, or her niece Catherine, her most faithful caller, to climb to her second floor flat, crowded with the things she had saved, her mother's things, the chinoiserie screen, Aunt Minnie's cows in a dark meadow, the sofa and chairs from the house on Cottage Grove Avenue, Great-grandfather Daniel's upholstered rocker, (each of the children ended up with one). There was a drawerful of rings—opals, garnets, onyx, the diamond ring of *pavé* brilliants set in a square. Grandfather Dirk had ordered three rings from Amsterdam when she and her sisters were young women, a square for Helene, an oval for Elizabeth, diamonds in the shape of a diamond for my mother, Esther Wilhelmina, who gave the ring to Mary Ellin when we were married.

Helene spoke with a crack in her voice followed by a dry little laugh which could indicate that she was either amused or amazed. Although there wasn't that much to be amused about as a daughter, as a sister, as an aunt, as a great aunt, and amazement was a thing of the distant past.

On her back verandah she stood among the pots of flowering plants waving goodbye for what always seemed to be the next to the last time, until she was no longer there. A puff, you turned your back, a puff and like the feathery head of a dandelion gone to seed, she was gone. And then there were none, except Uncle Bill who had done all the things Helene hadn't permitted herself to do and got away with them, back to home base with plenty of time to spare.

—⚍—

YESTERDAY THE LAST OF THE BARGAIN BULBS WENT IN, a dozen red botanical tulips. If I haven't been too late, three months from now they will break ground. By then we shall be in Sicily—another return, this one after thirty-five years, to the place where we spent the first six months of our married life. A magazine assignment will insure a five-week stay in decent hotels during the *primavera Siciliana.*

Mary Ellin has been on the phone with Mr. B. talking about her mother who says she doesn't feel up to any visits now, not even from her daughters. The doctor has told Mary Ellin it is hardening of the arteries. Mr. B. says only "If there was anything you could do, I'd drag you down here by the hair. Right now, there isn't. You know, you've tried. She won't see anyone."

Mary Ellin gives him messages. About the children, about Peter. "She has the pictures you sent," Mr. B. says. "She knows Elizabeth has a beautiful baby."

Mr. B. stands, I realize, at approximately the same distance from his first grandchild, Elizabeth, as I now stand from my first, Elizabeth's son Peter. How odd. There is so little in our two lives that is parallel. Certainly his experience of success has been very different from mine—his the absolute kind growing from an enormous and unique and inexplicable talent, a formidable energy—against my "at least" variety—"at least" I have not made *that* mistake, suffered *that* horror, while underneath was this other drive, the spiritual one, shoving me, grinding me on, guiding me past one potential disaster after another. Meanwhile the certifiable genius was making one song after another, words and music fitting together as though they never had been apart, nor ever would be again.

Not only has he written more songs, more memorable, it would seem, than anyone in history. Mr. B. has set some sort of record for, if not old age, acknowledged old age, having put himself flatly to it at sixty and persisting so far for four decades. There are not too many who can claim that. And what has been the value of all those years to him? He doesn't talk about it.

The old are like Indians—naturally noble, they have been degraded and put down. It is my concern to reinstate them to their former dignity. The nursing homes, geriatric wards, and SROs are the old folks' reservations where these once potent people are herded away from us and where they forget who and what they are and lose their mana.

Now as my father-in-law wrote: "Like the Seminole, Navajo, Kickapoo, like the Cherokee, I'm an Indian too." And so he is. And so am I.

Today it is raining a steady, stubborn grey rain, through grey leafless trees, but in this house it doesn't seem to matter. It is good to be here with Mary Ellin, the animals, the books, the chores, a set of galleys to correct, and the children at the other end of the phone. Success.

1988

1988_

NEW YEAR'S DAY. I've decided I agree with Salvador Dali. Every old person, like it or not, is a hero since heroism is quintessentially the conscious facing of death and holding firm. And that is what old age is about—the preparation for, the growing awareness of, the consciousness of that confrontation. In a way that is what life is about. But most of our heroes have been limited to the early and more obvious manifestations. Still, the writers of epics, the authors of the lives of the saints are right: However arrived at, a good death is the noblest product of life—the last possibility, the ultimate fruit, its final justification. Mountain climbers, explorers, drag racers, hang gliders, sky divers, Christian soldiers, all tyrant-defiers are analogues for this end—their training for, their flirting with, their defying of death (if indeed they don't achieve death early on), is a rehearsal for the real heroism to come.

—⚏—

YESTERDAY was Barbara K.'s annual winter party, a pantomime in celebration of persistence—everyone being thirty years older than when we first attended and if not strong, still going.

She lives in a pretty house in the East 90s, narrow and

it would seem mostly stairs. There are steep stairs to the door. Inside half the width of the house goes to stairs.

When we arrived people were tumbling down the stairs in great numbers as if to make their escape—past Skinny I., a big man, sitting at the top gesturing, rendering the passage still narrower. Below him, Eve A. was bundled into a cloak—a ghost of her exquisite acid self in the shadow of her dark wrap. Sally I., hair redder than God or the beautician intended, stood in the angle; behind her in the designated drawing room was chaos. Despite all those departing there was nowhere to hang our coats. Downstairs, upstairs on the stairs, all our friends and many more seemed to have gathered. Harold T., crushed into the balustrade, was being spun first one way and then the other by people seeking the bar, seeking the buffet, seeking the biffy. Max L. in animated conversation with Arthur S. squeezed into the wall to permit Mary Ellin still carrying our coats access to the third floor. Above them she pinned Hank L. into the bend as she climbed upward.

There was Liz S., Bowden B., Leila H., Harold L., George P., Russell H., David and Lee G., Douglas A., Lester K., Judy F., Norman M., Babs S., Paul M. The talk was fragmentary, communication mostly by signal not words—a lifted eyebrow, a shrug, an extended hand if you could reach it. The food and drink had become impossible to reach. Still everyone comes and will come to the summer party. There are two a year—same people, same crush. Endurance, patience, persistence—survival! More than survival, a kind of glorious defiance that brings us in one great chattering, dithering, protesting, triumphant mob to yet another landing. We've made it through another six months with Barbara at the top of the stairs greeting us and offering us more inaccessible food and drink.

—〰—

SINCE I CONTEND that old age has as many advantages as the earlier stages of life, I should be willing and able to prepare a list of these advantages for others, more skeptical than myself, to examine and judge. Like that old friend at Barbara's who asked me what I was up to. I confessed I had started a new book, a running commentary on getting old.

"Oh, *please*," she said, turning away.

"The *consolations* of old age," I said, trying to reassure her. But she, who had just undergone a highly successful face-lift, would not be reassured.

Of course, the advantages of old age are conditional (I am marshaling my arguments a day after the fact) upon a willingness to accept and enjoy them, even to allow that there may be as many at the end of life as at its beginning and in between.

For instance, at this time of life I believe that a perception of cause and effect should grow clearer and more exact. Not just in larger time frames but on a moment by moment basis so that nothing about life can be dismissed as insignificant—a party, a face-lift. Such a perception—which means milking each encounter, each event for its ultimate meaning—earlier in life would be inconceivable, or at least would be thought to induce an intolerable vertigo. The old know better. Those who can't acknowledge and employ this faculty should be considered unfortunate—just as those without looks and personality are pitied in youth, or those without success and respect in middle age.

And boredom disappears. Gerald used to refer to this as a signal advantage of the spiritual life—that you are never bored. In railroad stations, in dentists' offices, at tea or cocktail parties, in the endless waits of war, all those deadly voids can be filled with prayer. They become opportunities. The old may bore others but there is no need for them to be bored themselves.

Then there is the matter of sin. Running down the list of one's own possible sins and their status is never a waste of time. Envy may be in decline, but that was a process that began some time ago. Anger hangs on, albeit by a thin thread. The other sins have lost ground simply because of physical weakness, diminishing will, wandering attention. "We pride ourselves that we are leaving our sins; actually our sins are leaving us" is a useless saying, however true. Explaining away the decline of sin in old age, saying no one should take credit, serves no purpose. Yet, are we still after credit and praise and approval, an occasion to boast? Pride, the final peril. Clinging to pride we certainly shall, as John Donne fears, "Perish on the shore." I pride myself on the death of pride. More work left to do.

Another advantage of old age comes via Goethe: "One has only to grow older to become more tolerant. I see no fault that I might not have committed myself."

And Sir Thomas Browne adds this: "Confound not the distinctions of thy life which nature hath divided; that is youth, adolescence, manhood and old age; nor in these divided periods, wherein thou art in a manner four, conceive thyself but one. Let every division be happy in its proper virtues, nor one vice run through all. Let each distinction have its salutary transition and critically deliver thee from the imperfections of the former; so ordering the whole that prudence and virtue may have the largest section."

Today is the Feast of St. Cuthman who bumbled about seventh-century Britain looking for suitable employment, pushing his ancient mother in a wheelbarrow before him.

—ɯ—

ON TUESDAY I went to Bert Dagmar's mass at St. Patrick's. A Catholic friend had arranged it when he died fifteen months ago, that is how long the wait was. It was the 5:30 service—only three people there, as far as I could determine, honoring Bert. The friend who was responsible for the mass was absent, undergoing major surgery. Maybe forty or fifty others were present for regular afternoon communion. Still it was unquestionably Bert's service—his name mentioned twice—no one's else. A homily—suitable for any occasion. There was a note in the mini-missal saying who should and shouldn't take communion. I took it anyway.

Bert, a Jew, was celebrated in that exclusive place, at the high altar. A Jew, and I suspect, a gay Jew, although in all the years I knew him sex was never mentioned. The pictures on his walls were of himself: with a microphone, on stage in a tuxedo, as Al Jolson, his most successful routine— Jolson himself had come to see him and approve. And alongside pictures of the two identifiable women, Helen Morgan and Kiki Roberts, was a colored photograph of a nameless brunette, striking in shawl and mantilla, castanets aloft, looking out with a provocative half smile.

Knowing Bert, he was capable of letting on he was gay just for the little additional attention that it would buy him. Weekly visits from SAGE as well as WEME. Why not?

At any rate a splendid memorial was dedicated solely to him: He was heading the bill. The costumes, the lights, the music, the premises more elegant than the Roxy in its prime. The performance of his life and death. Show business. There is nothing, as my father-in-law has affirmed, like it.

Until you are old, or indeed until you acknowledge that you are old, which can be something quite different than the mere fact, it is possible to believe that you are on some sort of legitimate detour, that life itself is really made up of a series of such detours—some quite pleasant, others not so, a necklace of detours—with no indication of a main road. But being old involves the realization and acknowledgment that you are and always have been on the highway and now the destination is clear and unavoidable: To realize that early on in life and to hold firmly to your course would be enlightenment, sanctity. To bumble into it as Bert apparently did is the consummation most of us can expect. It is only a matter of time.

—◆—

DAUGHTER ELIZABETH and grandson Peter are here to visit us before we leave for Sicily.

It is difficult to think of Peter, our first grandchild, as the Hindus would, as an instrument of release. His impact is so light. Not that his overall impression *is* one of delicacy. He is now a sturdy nine-month-old—more handsome than pretty, but his connection with the outside world is delicate. His look is evaluative—serious and steady—who is this old fellow making odd noises and gestures at me? Then fluttering into a smile and gurgle, breaking into a crow followed by some physical gesture of his own—a wave of the arm or a scuttle across the carpet. Peter, whether bundled into his outdoor outfit, mittens and stocking cap, small face pink, just in from the winter park, or in his bunting, lying on my stomach eye to eye, gives me, his grandfather, more than one message, of love, of destination.

But there is definitely a distinction between the bond of one's own children and the bond of one's grandchildren: in my case, Elizabeth, the first hostage to fortune, and Peter, the first grandchild, a challenge and a release.

My own children. There are flashbacks of them very young: Elizabeth, rocking her playpen on the lower floor in Weston. Beyond the window is the shining brook that next season, after we had moved on, filled the room to its roof. Irving in his camel-hair coat and cap standing on the sidewalk in Westport, a wistful look on his three-year-old face; Mary Ellin, mischievous in the dappled shade of our Wilton lawn; Katherine in her pram bundled almost into invisibility against the Chicago winter. They are all looking up at the parent towering above them, waiting for the click, the blinding flash.

But soon they, our children, managed to obliterate, day by day, their former, dependent, questioning selves. Eventually they have taken off, one by one, leaving indelible glimpses of sudden needs, excruciating crises, moments of humor and pride that marked the older child, the teenager, the young adult. Cute, smart, pretty, stalwart, exasperating, infuriating, alarming, inspired, aspiring, lovable —they were and are, *au fond,* our children.

But this lovable, irresistible child, our grandchild, is someone else's. Only ours at one remove.

SICILY

SINCE THE LATE SPRING OF 1953 when we left Taormina for the last time I have returned there in dreams—more often than anywhere except Des Moines. Although the place is not always clearly identifiable as Sicily, some voice tells me it is—that same voice that identifies people and places in dreams, whatever their appearance may be. Or I manage to recognize it myself from a few salient details— the steep climb to get to the town, the antique crenelations on the buildings, the cobbled streets, the view from above down to the fishing coves where the multi-colored boats are drawn up onto the sand, the peasants, the cocks, the donkeys, the carts, the distant roar of traffic, and over all a great white floating presence with a plume drifting westward from its flattened peak, Mount Etna. Otherwise

it may bear no resemblance to Taormina at all. Still I know
I am back.

I wonder if I'll know I am back this time. The manner
of getting there will be so different. Instead of a slow boat
across the ocean and into the inland sea, then in our
Hillman Minx with the top down descending the boot of
Italy by easy stages, we'll have the narrowness of two
planes, the blighting uniformity of three airports—here,
there, and in between.

And after we get there finally, in truth, thirty-five years
later, how much will remain of the remembered Taormina,
the Taormina of dreams. What, after all, is the real
Taormina? At what point in its two thousand years, if ever,
was it real? When, if ever, did it turn from reality to illusion, and when return? Did we, young, wide-eyed, with
our lives before us, succeed in finally making it real? These
are intimidating questions, and more so when eventually,
as they must, they are turned on oneself. When in my sixty-
seven years have I been real enough to encounter a real
town, a real island, a real kingdom?

In the airport lounge awaiting departure I notice an Italian
gentleman, older, borderline distinguished—*professore, com-
mendatore, dottore,* or diplomat perhaps—in a hat, the only
hat in the crowded room. I immediately guess he is pro-
tecting his baldness. On the plane he is seated two rows
ahead of us in the best coach location, in the front row
where there is free space between him and the bulkhead.
He reads all night—and all night, his bald pate reflects the
light. Each time he shifts position, like a mirror in the sun,
he wakes me from whatever shallow sleep I manage.
Otherwise the flight is fine, if any flight can be fine. Having
pre-ordered the antipasto supper, Mary Ellin is instead given
the vegetarian plate; eventually, by successive refusals, she
ends up with lobster and *pâté* from Ambassador Class.

. . .

A white Fiat sedan is waiting for us at the Catania airport with a trunk large enough to store all our luggage out of sight so that the *cattivi ragazzi*, who break windows at traffic lights and grab anything visible, won't see it.

Catania, never an attractive town, at least on its margins, was hard to get out of. Along the shore, the Cyclopi, the great rocks thrown by the one-eyed giant at the fleeing Ulysses, are all but lost in the midst of a jumble of new hotels, restaurants, villas. Finally we are on the *autostrada* with one clear view of Castelmola, the medieval village perched on a peak at the end of our garden, now pinned to the sky by a double rainbow. A few tunnels more and we are in Taormina, the town on a shelf, as convincing as any dream.

Close up the carts are gone, the cocks, the donkeys, no bent old men in capes and caps, no old women in black on black, black shawls, black scarves, black dresses. The crowds on the Corso Umberto are trippers like ourselves or natives from the surrounding countryside in their weekend best.

The house we lived in thirty-five years ago, the Casa Talio, two rooms downstairs (small) and two rooms up (smaller) has grown to a substantial villa with a parlor large enough to accommodate two pianos comfortably. From the terrace, which is new, it is impossible to pick out the antique German musician's chalet on the once green hillside opposite. Nor can we see Fontana Vecchia, the scruffy villa where Lawrence and Frieda exchanged frying pans and rolling pins and Truman Capote spent a season with his Pekingese before his career really got under way. Both are lost in a steep slope of dusty condominiums and sickly pink and dirty white *casas*. Trees and underbrush now gone along with the cocks and the donkeys. At the far end of the narrow garden Castelmola rises above us ringed by tall tenements the color of machine-made sherbet, medieval village no longer.

Should these changes be such a shock? Since I began this account we have faced Seattle, Des Moines, California. Now it's Sicily out of control.

But from the front window the Campo Santo with its green-black cypress, the Ionian sea, purply blue, and the mountains of Calabria deep in snow are still there, and above the garden wall the convent bells ring as we remember them.

Confronted by Taormina Mary Ellin's response is to burst into tears. Standing at the nearly familiar front door of that tiny house, now weirdly enlarged, and confronted by the memory of us young, hopeful, refugees from *Time* and the privileges and hazards of postwar Manhattan, on our own for the first time in this ridiculously beautiful spot, she weeps. And back in our hotel room, tears again: sitting at the desk, she is honoring her commitment to write it all down. "Why don't *you* cry?" she asks in sudden anger.

"An old man sniveling is not attractive. And what are you crying about? Because we are no longer that good-looking bride and groom who were somewhat less innocent, more ambitious than they admitted? Because now we have four great blobby children, and a blobby grandchild? And are big blobs ourselves?" (At least regarding the children the description is unfair—they are better looking and more pulled-together than we ever were.) But I have made Mary Ellin laugh, which she usually does, even when my jokes are not all that funny. One of my duties in life it seems, for the past thirty-five years, has been to make my high-strung, quick-to-tears wife laugh.

We leave our hotel room, walk back up the Corso. There suddenly in the heart of Taormina, our honeymoon village, is one of the great squares of the world, the Piazza Nova Aprile, greater than the Place de la Condorde if only a fiftieth its size; it is greater than the Place Vendôme, San Marco, Picadilly Circus. On three sides are doll-size medieval buildings of centuries-weathered stone, and over its balustrade is a coastline stretching all the way to Siracusa and beyond, sloping up to Europe's most beautiful and sinister mountain, Etna, the gate to hell, spring's entry. It is an outlook to freeze your tears, to challenge your spirits.

For dinner it snows, large drifting flakes beyond the hotel windows. The dining room is filled with scandalized guests. Isn't this supposed to be the *primavera Siciliana*? Our waiter tells us tomorrow when we set out to circle the island it surely will be warm and sunny.

—〰—

IN AGRIGENTO, THE GRANDE HOTEL DEI TEMPLI, however scruffy, was the *albergo* of choice for travelers for a hundred years. There we figure Elizabeth, our eldest, was conceived at the moment the bed collapsed. The Hotel is no longer here. In its place is a school of archeology, with two hundred students plus faculty, marble floors, ordered gardens, newly plastered halls. But from our terrace at the Villa Athena, smaller, lower, closer, at seven A.M., the majestic Temple of Concord, across a shallow ravine, and up a short slope, has little changed since we last saw it—or for that matter in 2,500 years. At the moment, I have it and its companions stretched along the hill—the Temple of Juno, of Herakles, of the Dioscuri—all to myself.

No one has visited these honey-colored temples in a spirit of devotion for centuries. Still on the hill in the early morning sun, at midday, spotlit at night, there is something about them that can't be dismissed. It is not a message of mortality, of how the mighty have fallen, of the vanity of human wishes—there is no representation of man or beast or vegetable about those serenely proportioned Doric columns except over to the right—prone and out of sight, a plastic replica of a giant *teleman*. The gods that lived here once are gone, absconded. Nor would they be welcomed back. The message, the warning if you will, is for each of us.

What must you do to keep your particular god alive and in place? The answer is that there is nothing particular about God. Meanwhile the blue sky above and between, the persistent carpet of wild flowers, the pocked and crumbling stone make their hackneyed, their plangent comment.

Daedelus landed here in Earaclea Minoa on his flight from Crete. The aging Minos followed after and founded a city of which only a theater, high and commanding an incomparable view of Sicily's southern coast, remains, covered against the elements with a sheet of yellow plastic. The muted sun reminds us of Icarus who never made it. Perhaps it was just as well. Minos, once lord of the Mediterranean, become a frail old man, was scalded to death in his bath by the daughters of the local chieftan.

In Selinunte more wild flowers, more fallen columns, more echoes of dead rulers and gods, and in between the two silted harbors coveted by Carthage, beneath the tumbled acropolis, the beginnings of a beach resort.

Mary Ellin loses her red umbrella, a gift brought by a friend from Tokyo, carried the length of the Indian subcontinent from Katmandu to Bede Griffiths' ashram at Trichy. She threads her way back through the ruined temples and finds it bright against a heap of golden stones.

The small *museo* in Marsala is up a narrow flight of stairs. In it are eight magnificent tapestries and nothing else, depicting Vespasian and the destruction of Jerusalem. These hangings we are told were once the property of Philip of Spain and Mary Tudor, two bloody, bloodless bigots who in their own mindless way did their best, if unwittingly, to kill their god. Vespasian, bloody Mary, bloodless Philip—what's to choose? Jerusalem, I know for a fact and from experience, remains. As potent as ever.

A dozen older people are at Segesta. A tour bus waits in the large parking lot beside the gift shop *ristorante*. The last time it was just the almost perfect, not quite finished, temple in its bowl of hills and us with a picnic lunch. At the end of the afternoon a carload of French nuns climbed up the hill to take our place, in bright blue habits with wide starched hats like white coracles or the white clouds that had been marching across the sky all day.

The great Christ Pantocrators in Monreale, in Cefalu, in the Capella Palatina, are huge but in no way gross. Their glare, their hands, are they raised in blessing? Or in judgment?

What other effigies of God or his stand-in compare to these? The giant Buddha in Nara, the figures prone or upright in Polonnaruwa, the images traced on the earth in Machu Picchu, the animal-headed figures sitting or frozen in their timeless stride up the Nile? The Colossus of LeShan, or Mount Rushmore? I have seen none of them, and now probably never shall. But three Pantocrators should be enough.

Back in Taormina, my sleeping wife beside me, I lie in bed at the Villa Paradiso and stare at the tips of three giant cypresses stepped to the south, moving in a slight breeze. Behind them the sky is lemony and higher up a pale, pale blue. The iron railing that runs around our terrace marks the lower margin of my view, the scallop of our awning the upper. I sit up and there is the low misty slide of Etna, a gentle blue-grey only slightly deeper than the sky. Below it the curve of the Ionian shore is cluttered with the beach hotels of Naxos—still lit from the activities of last night. Beyond is a patch of green which marks the first Greek colony in Sicily, or for all I know, anywhere. A farther dimmer point is Catania—and beyond that the faint line above an almost indistinguishable horizon—maybe Syracuse, at one time the greatest city in the ancient world. I stand up and there is Etna—all of him (or her)—death—snowy and black with a plume (of cloud? smoke? steam?) blowing eastward from her/his cone. I am in Taormina on the first day of daylight saving time, in what must be the best hotel room in all the town which boasts hundreds of hotel rooms more luxurious than this. But there is no other room from which you can see, lying, sitting up in bed, all of that—remember all that—the beginning, the middle that it led to, perhaps what comes next.

Well, maybe there is the same bottomless backward spin from the Teatro Greco, invisible behind us, every tourists' destination, the subject of a thousand water colors, a million snaps. It is the locale of a melancholy description drawn for us by a literary friend, of André Gide, ancient as meerschaum, sitting on the theater's stone steps staring not out at Etna, the gate of Hades in all its magnificence, but down at a group of Sicilian youths at play on the ruined stage. The assumption is that he is looking down in regret, envy, or the dusty lust of an old man—or perhaps, one hopes, weary relief.

A bell rings. A family, father, mother, daughter, in their best clothes walks up the Via Roma. It is Palm Sunday, 1988. In a week we will be gone with another return unlikely.

But wait—Mary Ellin is awake, eating her breakfast, orange juice, strong coffee, and a bun. "Wouldn't it be great," she says around the pastry, "if we came back for our fiftieth anniversary? Bring the family, all of them. So what if you're in a wheelchair? They can push it. We can hire a couple of *raggazi cattivi* to carry you up the steps at Noto, at Enna, at the shrine of St. Rosalia. Peter, a sixteen-year-old, would love it."

NEW YORK

THAT LIFE IS some sort of monstrous pyramid scheme seems to be a common view among those approaching old age. You send off your ten dollar bill to the unknown name at the top of the list and then after mailing the requisite letters to friends and relations warning them not to break the chain, wait for nothing, wait all the way to death with declining expectations and the growing conviction that there are, after all, no winners.

More likely, if we pay attention, if we believe in Easter which is today, there are no losers. The cathedral was packed. We visited Mrs. B. sitting up in her four poster bed, the East River bright in the window behind her, Mary Ellin giving her the egg-shaped mother-of-pearl box we brought from Taormina.

Soon it will be May, the month of anniversaries and celebrations, my sixty-eighth, Peter's first, Mr. B.'s hundredth. May 13th Irving will have his art show at Elaine Benson's gallery, his first major display; on the 20th he celebrates his thirty-third birthday. The 17th would be Eddie's sixty-third were he alive; also it's the publication date for *Spare Days*. That is it for May. No, not quite. Katherine and Benjy's second wedding anniversary is the 31st and some time in the month will be my book party at the Grangers. Lee Granger reports that one hundred invitations have been sent, and no one, as yet, has said no.

And looking back, why not mention March 4, the day I died and returned, which happens to be Brother Dirk's birthday. In all that time that we have been brothers, sixty-eight years, there was never a serious falling out—a departure from the admiration in which I held him, nor any reason for a falling out, at least for me falling out with him, the admirable, lovable older brother. Nor can I recall, and this is even more mysterious, any envy. No wonder I chose his birthday for my round trip.

Mr. B. told Mary Ellin's sister Linda earlier this week that he hoped he would make it to the 11th, the great day, so he wouldn't let ASCAP, the society of composers he'd helped found, and their gala Carnegie Hall event, down. Earlier he had been quoted as saying gleefully the exact opposite—that maybe he would die before the date and scotch all that pretentious fuss. One declaration is as typical as the other—both laced with humor and a grain of salt. In your hundreth year you don't take such things too seriously; at least he doesn't, though others may.

He is apparently getting frailer and frailer but is still going downstairs. The elevator, Linda says, hasn't been checked or licensed in two years so he is traveling illegally between the floors in his own house.

Meanwhile Mrs. B., who a few months back had refused company of any sort, has sustained a stroke, perhaps more than one. She now has at least one of her daughters with her every day and last week welcomed a visit from her sister-in-law.

A *stroke*—another one of those deeply ambiguous words, with both meanings appropriate to the condition: the hand of God striking you quickly, decisively, unequivocally, or God by gentle gestures making the passage from here to there calmer, easier.

In some way the Berlins' house at 17 Beekman Place

has become an emblem of old age, of the terminal negotiation with mortality which now involves two people instead of just one, two people who could live for weeks or months or die tomorrow—literally living on the edge. Mrs. B.'s death would have as disastrous an effect on the celebration Wednesday night as would Mr. B.'s.

Mary Ellin noted that in the large piece about her father in the *New York Times* there was no mention of his wife of sixty-three years, nor his three children, nor his nine grandchildren, nor his one great-grandchild. It is as if his talent and the weight of years isolated and insulated him not only from the world at large but from his immediate family as well. Which in a way, I suppose they have.

WATER MILL

THE GUEST PREACHER at church announced we were heading into Old Folks Week (the first I'd ever heard of such a thing) and in place of a sermon read a piece by a member of the Episcopal Society for Ministry on Aging whose wife had Alzheimer's. "The disintegration of a vibrant personality, a companion and loved one for many years, is tragic to watch," this remarkable old man begins. "Sixty-four years of a loving and happy marriage seem to go out the window when she looks at me and says. 'Who are you? Where is my husband?'" He ends, "As we go down that inexorable road together, I pray that a merciful Father will leave me here until we reach the end, and that when it comes, mine will be the last loved face she sees, mine will be the last reassuring voice she hears . . ." His is a valid reason, perhaps the only one, for praying to outlive someone else, no matter how old you are, or how feeble.

. . .

When we grow old we all become Japanese—one beautiful object, a flower, a picture across a room to focus on is enough—or the moon, a tree, with or without leaves. Last night it was the sickle moon and the evening star beside it, and before that a sunset with all the colors of a faded rainbow leaching out of it, stripes without stripes across a pale, pale sky.

—m—

HOW DO YOU CELEBRATE your father-in-law's hundredth birthday, a birthday you never thought you'd make, not because you doubted for a minute that he would stay the course, but because you—thirty-two years his junior—were shaky? But here we are, both him and me, still around for the big celebration. May 11th, the very day, it rains, pouring rain. I, the oldest son-in-law, a different kind of old, bring in the morning *Times* at seven, and there to help me to get on target is an editorial marking the event.

I tune in the TV, choosing arbitrarily "Good Morning, America"—ABC seeming to me the network most likely to rise to the occasion. They do so with a double segment, the first dedicated to clips of memorable moments featuring my father-in-law's songs—well chosen. And there they all are, the dead and the alive, the forever young and the hardly ever old, Bing and Rosemary and Danny, Fred and Ginger and Judy, Al Jolson singing "Blue Skies," "Putting on the Ritz" from *Young Frankenstein*, Mr. Berlin himself singing "Oh How I Hate to Get Up in the Morning" and "God Bless America." And that is just the first segment. The second is a panel to discuss how great he was—Tony Bennett representing the singers, Tommy Tune the dancers, Isaac Stern the classical community—all eloquent and sincere— Stern saying the genius was like Mozart's, unselfconscious, inevitable. He is right.

. . .

In the evening the family members are all properly attired, and appropriately seated in the third row center at Carnegie Hall watching the best ASCAP could provide—some young, some not so young, some quite surprisingly old. Leonard Bernstein, an acknowledged fan—hadn't he devoted the better part of an early edition of *Omnibus* to "Watch Your Step," the first Berlin book-musical?—incoherently fights a battle in front of everyone which has nothing much to do with the occasion—or maybe more than was allowed. Shirley MacLean, happy as always, sings "Let Me Sing and I'm Happy"; Natalie Cole in blinding white belts out "Suppertime"; Willie Nelson trundles out a clutter of electronic gear for "Blue Skies"; Madeline Kahn is adorable (is she ever otherwise?) with "You'd Be Surprised"; and so on and on to a clutch of buddies in uniform from *This Is the Army*. All this is still barely scratching the surface.

Mr. B., we assume, is watching it all on closed circuit TV on the fifth floor at Beekman Place. The nation will see a delayed and edited version with appropriate sponsors sometime later.

Afterwards there is the banquet. Kitty Hart gorgeous at seventy-seven in lipstick red, points out that not only is today the hundredth birthday of a great man, but within the week, the great man's first great-grandson will celebrate his first birthday. This last fact I had insisted be put before the assemblage, the horde of dressed-up people in the hotel ballroom celebrating the celebration.

At midnight, a group of devotees had arrived at the house on Beekman place for a birthday serenade. Mr. B. got up, put on his bathrobe and prepared to descend and acknowledge their presence, offer them a hot drink as he had the year before. The nurses prevented it. Though the top window was lit, the singers finally went away uncertain whether they had been heard. They had. And two floors below Mrs. B. slept on, oblivious to them and the general celebration alike.

> *Since I am coming to that holy room*
> *Where, with the choir of saints forevermore*
> *I shall be made thy music, as I come*
> *I tune the instrument here at the door,*
> *And what I must do then, think here before.*

What would Mr. B. the non-believer, in his extremity—one hundred years, whatever your state of health, must be considered extreme—think of such a statement by John Donne, another precise lyricist softened by sickness and the proximity of death?

I can recollect just two Berlin songs that had anything to do with the subject. Maybe three, the last more than fifty years ago. Nothing since.

As a postscript to all the May fanfare, Mr. B. calls about Irving and the sales that he had made at his art show. In the past if you asked Mr. B. about his health he never admitted to feeling anything but worse. This time he volunteers he is feeling better. Nothing about his hundredth birthday or himself—he brushes that off—it is all about Irving and how great it is for him to have his talent confirmed, about his own conviction that Irving is probably the most talented member of the family, not excepting himself, and how he prizes the two or three pictures which Irving had given him. I hang up deeply moved. For a number of reasons I suppose; but principally for him, that at one hundred with all that hullabaloo going on around him, his principal enthusiasm and joy is for a grandson he hasn't seen in months.

—⁓—

THEY HAVE SUGGESTED AT THE CATHEDRAL that I deliver the Father's Day sermon to mark the publication of *Spare Days*. I declined and offered to read the Old Testament lesson instead. Job 38: The Lord saying to Job out of the tempest: "Brace yourself and stand up like a man; I will ask questions and you shall answer."

I read it loud and slow, as though I knew exactly what it meant and how it applied to me. Then I went back to the front row where a group of friends and relations, alerted to the occasion, sat.

Next came the sermon delivered by Jim Morton. After a few sentences he began reading from *Spare Days* and the remainder of his homily, perhaps twenty minutes, though it seemed much longer, was devoted to reading from my book. I don't know how other writers would have reacted to hearing their words read in the company of Job's and St. Paul's and St. John's in this vast place consecrated to the word of God. I sat very still, bent, as though expecting a deserved blow, even though in Jim's reading my words sounded much better than I remembered them—the negotiation with my disease, the doubts, the fears, the respite in Assisi, the jolt and affirmation at the end. I hadn't realized just how many affirmations I had been brash enough to make, enough at least to fill a sermon—or to invite God's judgment.

Now I must await the judgment or the indifference of others. Either way, I suddenly realized, this book really matters. More, given all my theories about old age, than it should.

WATER MILL

THERE WAS A SINGLE STAR VISIBLE in the western sky next to a scattering of clouds that like pieces of a puzzle moved slowly to the north over the potato fields. I had taken

Molly out for her final turn in the backyard in Water Mill and it was almost dark, but not quite, although already past nine. And facing that single star I thought as I haven't in years: "Star light, star bright, first star I've seen tonight, I wish I may, I wish I might, have the wish I wish tonight." And suddenly perhaps for the first time in my entire life (reciting that verse began early) there was no wish waiting for me. Nor would I risk one for my children or my grand-children, present or due to come. And I recognized the blank there in the sky behind the star as a gain for all of us.

Earlier the drawling voice on the weather phone, and the spiffy young man on the evening news had been telling us all hell is breaking loose—has broken loose—yet again. With the promise of torrential rains—winds—tornadoes—hail. But here, right here in our backyard with the self-sown foxglove, the iris and the columbine, the wild roses in bloom below that single star, all was calm and wish-free.

TWO ROOSTERS since mid May have taken possession of our property, one caparisoned in white with a glossy black underbody, the other dark with V's of white on the wings and the blue-black tail feathers favored on turn-of-the-century ladies' hats. I saw them first at the corner of Blank Lane and Scuttle Hole Road pecking away, and supposed that they had escaped from some nearby farm. Within a day or two one had gravitated to a neighbor's yard, the other—the one with the cape of white feathers—to ours. At this point it was assumed that they were vagrants—homeless pets that had been left off, as dogs and cats are at the end of the summer, by feckless renters. Since they never had the look of proper barnyard fowl, we theorized that they might be fighting cocks or ornamental specimens.

By now they are both on our property, nesting in the mulberry tree and waking at five to peck and noisily crow under our windows. Molly is troubled but stays clear. Pippo, a cat generally fatally interested in birds, watches but does not pounce since the two of them would make one and a half of him. Irving says, either they go or he goes. I am not bothered because they crow on the other side of the house and besides I am deaf, another advantage of old age. But how do you rid yourself of them if you want to?—and I am not sure I want to. They aren't edible, they aren't catchable, and there is indeed something endearing about the vain, mindless creatures. I have already bought them a bag of cracked corn at Agway and put a pan of water beyond the shed in the hopes of tempting them out from under Irving's window.

It occurs to me as I am eating breakfast and listening to the roosters that the two great commandments—to love God and to love our neighbor as ourself—make no obvious accommodation for enemies or for those who are simply inconvenient. We assume that we ourselves are lovable. But what about God? That He is lovable we must take on faith but the suspicion that He, along with all too many of our neighbors, is against us—is hard to overcome. Suspicion of this negative sort is undoubtedly what distinguishes enemies from friends and lovers, the kind of suspicion that is the intrusive, pervasive instrument of the devil. Love is our means of defeating it. God is love. Loving love and all His creation must be our salvation. If we see God as the enemy (and a lot of us do, sporadically or continually), to see God as love is the challenge, not an excuse. "Brace yourself and stand up like a man" as the Book of Job would have it.

All this above the crowing of the cocks. Indoors, sitting down at the typewriter, I hear Irving's impatient tread overhead. The day is under way.

—⚬⚬⚬—

LAST NIGHT we had an early dinner with the Lerners. Edna is going in next week for exploratory surgery for a possible malignancy. She has read *Spare Days* twice and had a copy for me to sign for Paul Cowan, who is having a bone marrow transplant in Boston. The conversation was of cancer, a subject with the Lerners, like baseball, movies, real estate or the stock market might be with others we know. Michael, their eldest son, has just finished a report for some government agency on alternative therapies and has signed to write a book-length version. He has made himself, thanks to a MacArthur Grant, the preeminent authority on this topic. Max is halfway through his own book on his illnesses, at least two of them cancer, and cited passages from it. I find I have little left to say on the subject.

As for old age: Max had just delivered a talk at his sixty-fifth Yale reunion—fifteen survivors present with their wives and attendants. They were mostly deaf—so what he had to say, which Edna reported was splendid, fell on deaf ears—not deaf indifferent or hostile—deaf deaf. The speech which started with "Sailing to Byzantium" ended with Thomas Hardy's "An Ancient to Ancients." (Already quoted.)

Another dinner, this one at Dorothy and John Sherry's with Bill Gaddis and Muriel Murphy. A resolutely secular evening except that John's devotion to Alfred North Whitehead substitutes for religion and I don't know how resolute Muriel is in her disbelief. Bill and Dorothy, however, appear to be holding fast to their proud faithlessness, regardless of old age's approach.

At table the conversation was desultory literary—trashing Tennessee Williams and Lanford Wilson. There was a discussion of Chevy Chase in *National Lampoon's Vacation*, with Bill describing with relish extended portions involving a dead dog and a dead mother-in-law in the back seat of the family station wagon. Also we heard bits about the reading Bill is doing for his new book, a hilarious section of which was in the same issue of the *New Yorker* as the last chapter of *Spare Days*. There was retro talk of Aldous Huxley and Gerald Heard and their part in the drug culture . . . John had just read an account of their proselytizing activities in the fifties and sixties. I held my peace. Lately, at dinner tables not my own, I tend to listen to others holding forth even when I would seem to know more than they do about the subject at hand. Except, of course when, with the garrulousness of the old, I say too much. This wasn't one of those evenings.

As we left John handed me Whitehead's *Adventures of Ideas,* pointing out that toward the end of the book there was an eloquent statement describing fame as a halfway house which, considering the conversation and the company, might be taken as a commentary on the evening.

I am willing to believe that unbelief if persisted in—and I know untold numbers of aging unbelievers such as those at the Sherry's dinner table—will bring one to an understanding or at least a relationship with reality that is the equivalent of the most elaborate and detailed religious faith. There are many shortcuts to God even for those who don't realize where they are heading.

The fact is there is no getting away from Him. The absence of God is God—no God is God. The people who deny God are only saying that someone else's idea of God neither pleases nor satisfies them. It is God who allows them to deny Him. The inescapability of God is the nature of the world—the blind spot in every philosophy, in every alternate explanation, is God—that shadow of indeterminacy that hangs over everything is God's shadow. Chaos is God. God is inescapable. God or Whoever He is standing in for. So just as we are all equidistant from death, we all are or will be equally close to God.

—⚏—

EDNA CAME OVER IN THE AFTERNOON looking hale and chic in a pale grey-green linen suit. Although her operation revealed a malignancy, her lung X-ray was clear. She is going in next week for a complete CAT scan and has told Max not to interfere with the process. She obviously places herself somewhere between Max's aggressive mode—"I will or maybe I won't"—and a simple flowing with it, when it comes to her negotiations with her doctors and her cancer. She is prepared for them not to find out where the malignancy is coming from, for the mystery to persist.

Steve and Mary Ellin, Jr. had invited her to come with them to Paris in September and she has said yes. Now, she wasn't sure she wouldn't prefer to buy a Geoffrey Beene dress. She can't afford both. Hers was anything but a gloomy conversation although the news a week ago sounded ominous indeed. For a while she had thought seriously about death and the disposition of her belongings—how she would divide up her jewels and what would happen to the house, etc.— but that apparently didn't last long.

After she left, Mary Ellin and I talked about the moment in life when death becomes real to you. Mary Ellin seemed to think of it as a number, maybe sixty-five, more likely seventy, although she mentioned the impact of the loss of Harriet Gibney at age forty-eight, Tommy Murray at fifty-two, and especially Minda whom, she told me for the first time, she had seen dressed for the grave. This viewing of death—not accepting it but realizing its nearness—she obviously sees as a crucial yet shocking and depressing thing. For me, although I can't claim I often live up to this conviction, grasping the inevitability of death should be a release, a realization that doesn't depress but sets me free. That recognition that we are always at the same distance from death—all of us, whatever our age and condition— should make us more attentive, more alive. Maybe what

Mary Ellin means is that when we are old that realization is both easier and more threatening.

But when are we old? When we realize we are going to die? Is that the touchstone? Except we can realize the fact of death as a child. I certainly did. Mary Ellin didn't. Is it a matter of being able to hang on to the conviction if you have it, of not losing it as most people do early in life, when they forget it, push it aside? Even in war, in catastrophe, we can see ourselves as the survivor, the only survivor up until the last split second. We must accept death and then go on. And what is the significance of the experience I had when I "died" and then came back? It is puzzling . . .

—⁓—

THE SIXTIETH ANNIVERSARY of Eddie's death. At least I have always assumed that he died instantaneously on that hot July afternoon and not in the early morning hours on the following day. The scene at 1408 Forestdale with Mother prostrate in her bedroom, Dirk beside her, and me standing silent, watching, frozen in that black void beyond disbelief, and Poppa elsewhere, doing what had to be done—all that took place on July 2nd.

July 2nd here in Water Mill bears no resemblance to that hot humid Iowa day sixty years ago. It is cool and cloudy with a substantial breeze and in this cheerful house with its wide lawn and garden in full bloom death seems remote. Still my dark mood yesterday could have had something to do with the date, like a near-fatal rattlesnake bite that reproduces its symptoms year after year, and not have had to do with the full moon or an upset stomach or some delayed disappointment about my book—not enough sales, not enough praise. I keep hoping that somehow these dips, whatever their explanation, will fill in, level out as I grow older; but they don't.

"Sufficient unto the day is the evil thereof" is a text for

the young rather than the old. There is no more evil ahead then than now although if one wished to cavil one would say it is closer, later, and there is no longer in old age the time beyond that youth imagines will give one the opportunity to recover one's balance. But that isn't what I think Christ meant. What He meant was that the good of the day is also sufficient—that false hopes are as counter-productive as false fears and that hope should be general rather than specific. Which brings one to "Thy will be done" and faith and the parable of the talents. And so we totter through Matthew acting his gospel out day by day . . .

And my young mother lies groaning on her bed with the ruffled coverlet, in the room with the spotless starched muslin curtains, for all eternity, however long that may be, her baby gone but not forgotten—never, so long as I live, forgotten.

"Whom the gods love, dies young"—that often quoted line from Menander keeps coming back to me as some sort of excuse, justification. But such a statement is beyond proof. Once the plural gods give way to the singular, God's love becomes inscrutable. Its inscrutability seems its salient characteristic—the one that makes it endurable. If it were scrutable we'd all be born cinders—blasted at birth.

—⟊⟊—

"IF YOU TAKE A FAT LADY TO PORTUGAL you must bring her back." That was the inscrutable message buried some-where in last night's dream—made with singular emphasis, no attributable point of origin—a compelling inner voice. The dream itself had to do with painting the pillars on the porch at 1408 Forestdale. I fell asleep while painting, sleep within sleep. When I awoke to resume the task, I was over-whelmed with a sense, not that I wouldn't complete it, but that I would never properly begin. That sense of being mired in hopelessness frequently invades my dreams these nights but never my waking hours.

At seven I set the sprinklers in the pear trees and the vegetable garden. In the back it was still, a bright green stillness—the green moist, not yet beginning to dry out either from the season or the time of day. No birds—no breeze. Still—very still.

—⁓—

THE CALL CAME late yesterday afternoon that *Mrs. B.*, not Mr. B., was dying. On the kitchen counter was a stack of typed pages, our article "Sicily Revisited," with Mary Ellin's note: "Finally. It is just right. I am taking a shower."

I shouted through the bathroom door above the rush of water, "It's your mother's nurse. Your mother has taken a turn for the worse." The rhyme made the news seem even more ominous.

We drove into town in the middle of a heat wave and I was sent on home, being old, being sick myself, a heart patient subject to heat, to stress. Thus I was spared the seizures, the arrival of the priest, the doctor, the second doctor, the rush to the hospital, and finally the informing of Mr. B.—the real, the painful accompaniments of death.

NEW YORK

THOUGH THE HEAT WAVE PERSISTS, I am permitted to attend the funeral. The procession down the center aisle of St. Patrick's Cathedral of women in black: the daughters, Mary Ellin, Linda and Elizabeth, with the grandchildren. Our own Elizabeth has come from California, Mary Ellin, Jr.

and Steve from Washington. The Emmets from Paris, Irving, Katherine and Benjy, the Peters are already at hand. Many men in dark suits and black ties, the sons-in-law, the grand-sons-in-law, also the nephews and nieces, grand-nephews and grandnieces. The nave is filled with family, friends, curiosity seekers; there is a crush on the porch and around the great doors hoping to glimpse the hundred-year-old man who is now bed-ridden and not able to attend. If he *were* able, it would have been very different—simple, out-doors at the cemetery. What would an old Jew, he would certainly ask, be doing in this place?

Among the dozen con-celebrators are Father Laurence McGinley, once president of Fordham University who over-saw Mrs. B.'s return to the church and Cardinal O'Connor, hearty, in his Irish prime, who makes a last minute unsched-uled appearance. The music is undistinguished: the retreat slow back up the aisle behind the closed coffin. Curious eyes ignored, we mill about among friends and well-wishers on the Cathedral steps and ride in a half dozen limousines to Woodlawn where the grave has been opened beside that of the Berlin's infant son, dead on Christmas Day 1928 at three weeks, another ghostly child, never forgotten.

Finally we return to Beekman Place where one by one the children and the grandchildren gathered in the library go up to the top floor to greet the old man—who has out-lived his beloved wife, his last and principal companion.

"Enough," he finally says, "Enough."

So the last but one who can contradict the fact that I am old with any authority—who wished to hang on to the priv-ilege of keeping me in my place in a younger generation and exercised that privilege successfully to the end—is gone and my phoney, imposed youth with it. Now there is only a frail old man between me and—not old age—between me and It, whatever It may be.

MAR VISTA

WE ARE BACK WITH THE YOUNG in California. I set out for the church at ten and am the first but two in the sanctuary. The gospel is Matthew 25: "If you do it to the least of these . . ."—a text which has pursued me through most of my life. The sermon, delivered with notes, begins with a substantial reference to the World Series now in progress hereabouts, and wanders on until it reaches the final anecdote concerning an elderly neighbor of the pastor's. When the old woman died the family's only request was that the music for her funeral include "I'll Be Loving You, Always" (the song which Mr. B. gave Mrs. B. as her wedding present.) The poor old parishioner had taken up the piano at an advanced age and this was the favorite of all the tunes she had picked out. At first Father Fred demurred, saying he felt the song inappropriate for the organ. But during the night it came to him that the sentiments expressed in "I'll Be Loving You, Always" were, after all, profoundly religious. At the funeral, as the coffin was rolled down the center aisle, the organist (not at the organ, however—at the keyboard of the grand piano at the crossing) played "I'll Be Loving You, Always." And everyone's requirements were met, sort of.

Perhaps we would all have felt better if they had played that song at St. Patrick's for Mrs. B., Mr. B. present after all.

Now Mary Ellin and I have been left for a week with Peter, eighteen months, while Elizabeth and Sasha take a trip to New Orleans. It is their first break, our first stint as baby sitters, the primary duty of old folks in America in the eighties. Forget about retreating to the forest, the mountains, the seashore, unless of course you intend to take the grandchildren with you. Actually it is very pleasant.

We have Peter all to ourselves almost; a good-looking young Brazilian *au pair* is here to back us up. Elizabeth and Sasha seem less nervous, less intrusive, more competent than we were at their age. Fewer detailed instructions as they leave.

Peter, a Barrett blonde with a round head and sturdy body, is a new and energetic walker who needs watching. There is a fall due to inadequate supervision on our part followed by a terrifying wail. Examination reveals a scraped knee, treated and bandaged, but no concussion, no broken bones. There is also a "disappearance"— Peter and the *au pair* off without warning to join her buddies at the local mall. An abduction? Halfway to Rio by now? They return looking sheepish, Peter's face smudged with chocolate.

WATER MILL

CALIFORNIA HAS BECOME OUR "COMMUTE." In the past it has been a vacation, a place of pilgrimage, an object of eager anticipation, of fantasy. Now we come to sit. If not to sit, to follow, to fret, and occasionally to pursue. And after a lively week, we return home—which at this time of year is neither the forest nor the mountains, nor indeed the sea— but the potato fields of Water Mill. And to another funeral.

This funeral is Uncle Willie's: John William Mackay, Mary Ellin's favorite, her mother's younger brother, forever cheerful and affectionate, named for the formidable gent who made the family fortune and built the Greenwood mausoleum with the million-dollar view where the last of that generation of Mackays is now put to rest. All except for Aunt Gwen, Willie's wife of fifty-nine years who, though deep in grief, shows no signs of dilapidation. She will before long be back, one suspects, on the tennis court, shooting in Ireland and Wales, bucking up the next generation, setting an example.

Each of these departures, these divestitures (as we grow older they become alarmingly frequent) puts the question of survival in a more concentrated and intimate form and makes my own return still more mysterious. Nor do they solve the question of ultimate destination.

Wise and holy Jacob Boehme, the seventeenth-century shoemaker-visionary, thinks we go nowhere, we remain in place as in a giant aspic. The Buddha said there were as many destinations as there are travelers and choices, which means there is, after all, only one. Two views—one truth.

—⚶—

THE DAY BEFORE YESTERDAY had been one of anxiety—portal to portal. Finally last night the gloom lifted. From two A.M. on an encounter, an opening—not a crack, but as though one whole side of my habitation were blown away—and there I was, exposed to the elements, not shivering, not cowering, but acknowledging that there was no way to escape, and that those elements were the facts of life. The clutter I had gathered around me, perhaps in hopes of protection, was beside the point—not justification for either guilt or greed, for clinging or clutching or rejecting.

I have, it seems, been accumulating the pressure for this blowout over a period of weeks or even months since my mother-in-law's death—the trip to California to see the Matsons, a brief respite—then Uncle Willie's funeral.

And now in the midst of the blast, of this opening out, is an image, vivid, unmistakable—a face floating against that dark void, neither friendly nor unfriendly, though urgent and demanding. Not Piero's Christ, nor Monreale's—my own. A vision? I've never had one before. Two exposures—once—then again. Then gone.

. . .

Last night before I turned out the light on my side of the bed I told Mary Ellin that if you are in the bed you can't see what is under it. It was a comment on my concern that Molly might have slipped under the bed rather than out the door. But it was intended to mean more, another way of saying you can't describe the truth if you are embedded in it as we all—good and bad, smart and stupid—are. This is the reason why the ultimate particle, the outer limits of the universe, or any system at all, is never pinned down or satisfactorily closed.

Or maybe it is, as June at the Penny Candy Store says, the season. More people die, says June, in the fall—the season of decline. The angle of the year increases and the old and the ailing slip over the edge, and the rest of us—trying to hold them back, to keep from slipping ourselves—grow weary in spirit.

And at the end of prayers this morning, the long list of intercessions I go through each day before I open my eyes, it seemed there was a rough black surface, like a black shag rug, but with deeper pile, and in the center an opening, a circle drawing away like the shutter of a camera—a void turning slowly into a mirrored surface. I was staring into it, but this time there was no one staring back.

NEW YORK

TODAY I WAS ON THE GERALDO SHOW. Geraldo, Jerry Rivers, an acquaintance from Columbia, a two-time DuPont winner for his hard-bitten investigations of drug peddling in the South Bronx and of a desperately understaffed mental hospital on Staten Island, is now something else.

If the near-death experience, the subject of the show, is open-ended (as all we participants this afternoon would bear witness to and all but a handful of the audience would concur), this upper room, a half-block off Broadway and 42nd Street, must be the ultimate blind alley. There are no windows here. The bleachers are stacked to the back wall, packed with people who have nothing better to do and are dressed for the occasion. The light—we all confessed to the light—is merciless, glaring, without effulgence.

The primary participants are now being led to their chairs on the platform. I am planted in the audience, ostensibly to give the affair respectability. In a business suit, no makeup. The three so far on stage are all in pancake, young with square faces, one with glasses, one in a bright sweater. Dr. Moody, the expert, likewise in glasses, is brought in after warm-up instructions from a young, wisecracking producer on how to applaud, how to shout and whistle. "These guys were dead. Do they look dead?" "No!"

The panel is attached to their lavalier mikes. The camera lights come on. We are on the air, or at least "live on tape." And finally Geraldo, compact, handsome in his natty grey suit, the T-shirt investigative reporter turned circus ringmaster, enters to wild applause, shouts, whistles, and the show begins.

The panel is introduced: Tom Sawyer, the man in the sweater who had been crushed under a two-ton truck and wiped out for fifteen minutes, another young man who fell (jumped?—it is never properly explained) from a third floor window, another with a similar horror story I can't recollect—all are apparently very healthy and fit. Phyllis, a Gloria Steinem look-alike, is brought on stage; she is another expert who has written her own book on the travails of those who have to readjust to the "near-death" experience. She has had three of her own. She is very "up." Can she be *on* something? Or is it just the normal excitement of being *on* "Geraldo"?

I am introduced from where I sit in the first row. A note of sanity; a seasoned reporter; a teacher; a writer of books. The jacket of *Spare Days* is flashed on the screen. Old? Certainly I am the oldest of the show's participants. But in this case old has nothing to do with it. I give my account— how I went, how I came back, what happened in between. More applause, more shouts and whistles.

I observe that none of my fellow revenants mention the fruits of their experience in good works, in love of their fellow men, although they reported quite emphatically that they saw *God*.

In Times Square where my subway awaits me the night's activities have begun.

—⟁—

YESTERDAY, THE DAY AFTER CHRISTMAS, on the Feast of Stephen, we took our nieces, Rachel Peters and Emily Fisher, along with Mary Ellin, Jr. and Steve to a matinée of the *Nutcracker*. There was a message on the answering machine when we got home that Mr. B. had had a stroke which paralyzed his left side. We went to Beekman Place. He is unconscious.

Now a watch of sorts is on. So far Mr. B. hasn't regained consciousness. He is being fed by tube since they can find no veins for an IV. The purpose, the doctor tells us, is not necessarily to prolong life but to make him as comfortable as possible. Mary Ellin goes over in the morning and she or Elizabeth stays till evening just to be on hand. He recognizes no one. Linda is coming today.

Three days and we will have a New Year.

1989

1989

NEW YEAR'S DAY at Hannah Loewy's, a friend from the Cathedral of St. John the Divine: a half dozen of us crowd into one end of her living room facing a monumental clutter of stacked papers and books on chairs, on tables, on the floor. Richard Howard, the poet, is on one side; on the other is Dan Berrigan, the priest—a pleasant face, clear and peaceful with the shine of innocence about it, as though the seventies had never happened. Howard makes literary conversation; Berrigan is silent. There isn't a right moment to tell him how moving I found the memoir of his stint as an orderly at St. Rose's Hospice, a document to inspire and humble anyone who might pay an occasional visit to the old and sick.

Mr. Berlin's decline seems gentle compared to the agonized departure of those anonymous men ravaged and isolated by cancer—he's lying there in his own house, with his own nurses and daughters, and his doctor's daily attendance. Are these ministrations the equivalent of Father Berrigan making your bed, taking out your slops, mopping your brow, holding your hand, saying your prayers, listening to your protests, your lonely shouts of pain, giving you the final blessing? Who's to say?

. . .

Mr. B. spoke the day before yesterday. "I'm cold," he said, coming out of the coma he had been in since the day after Christmas. A sort of recovery seems to be taking place although yesterday he said nothing.

Margaret, one of Mr. B.'s nurses, says his condition is one of almost imperceptible frailty, as if the thread holding him to life were stretching, not necessarily tauter, but finer and finer with only the gentlest of indications of his being aware and responding—no words, nor looks really, maybe a returned pressure of the hand.

And with Mr. B.'s example before me, perhaps because of it, I still, every day, entertain the notion that this day, for me as well, could be my last. Upon consideration this may seem an affront, an attempt to claim for myself some unwarranted attention. Except that the claim—that death is always there adjacent, a split second away—is the same for me and every other living creature. And why not let the slow dying of someone near and dear remind us of our own mortality? In childhood a reminder of that possibility came from Isaac Watts' wildly inappropriate prayer recited nightly by those least likely to die before they awoke, followed by a long list of childish blessings.

Mr. B., at 101 on the very lip of eternity, may have no sense of death's imminence or his own precariousness. It has become the element he swims in—swims or treads water.

Today is the Feast of the Presentation in the Temple—Old Folks Day—Holy Simeon, Anna, and the *nunc dimittis.* Simeon who had hung around for years, finally released:

> *Lord, now lettest thou thy servant depart in peace,*
> *   according to thy word:*
> *For mine eyes have seen thy salvation*
> *Which thou hast prepared before the face*
> *   of all people;*

*A light to lighten the Gentiles, and the glory of
thy people, Israel.*

Day by day Mr. B. gains strength. He is now sitting up and
speaking.

An odd dream. I am in bed in Grandmother's living room
on Rosecrans in San Diego and am awakened by a strange
presence standing over me at bedside—a tall, thin figure
that grows taller and thinner as I look up at him. He has a
loose disarranged collar and mysteriously resembles Ensign
Miller—a puffy, flabby friendly fellow-officer in Seattle and
in the New Hebrides, whom I haven't even thought of in
forty-five years, not tall nor thin at all. The figure speaks.
"I am death," he explains and repeats the words. I wake or
half-wake in alarm.

Tomorrow it will be six years since I died in truth.

—◊◊◊—

YESTERDAY MARIAN MURPHY, a slender woman of uncertain age with a beautiful burnished face shared the pulpit
at the Cathedral with me. The billing was "Two Cathedral
Testimonies. Raised to a New Beginning."

Five years ago I had dreamed I was doing just this, walking down the nave, climbing the pulpit steps between the
figures of John the Baptist and Moses, looking out across
"a vast sea of faces." Struck dumb, I wept.

This time, as in the dream, vested in a crimson robe,
in a procession led by the choir, four crosses, the thurifer,
the gospeller, four candle bearers, assorted clergy and the
Dean, I walked with Marian to the row of chairs beneath
the pulpit.

Marian mounted the steps first. "On a tranquil September afternoon in 1975 in New Orleans," she began, "my

daughter Ingrid was abducted, raped, and murdered." She went on in her clear, musical voice to tell the terrible story; the discovering of her eight-year-old daughter's body, the apprehending of her murderer—the young white man who lived with his wife and two daughters next door, the destruction of her own marriage as a result of the tragedy. She also spoke of her life before the tragedy. One of a heroic group of youngsters who had desegregated the Baton Rouge schools, Marian had risen out of the isolation and hostility of her childhood to become a successful professional woman, happily married, family begun. And then the horror—and the long struggle that followed—a woman in the midst of life floundering and slowly miraculously recovering.

"It is grace that can make a new beginning," were her concluding words. "It is grace that makes it possible to laugh and love again."

Marian came down from the pulpit and I mounted in her place. Tears would have been appropriate or, at the least, silence. But, for better or worse, I had contracted to deliver my testimony of survival—life after "death"—faith after "death." I spoke my piece, however perfunctory, however mundane, and went back down the steps to my assigned place and the service proceeded under the pall cast by Marian's tragedy. God poses some questions that no glibness, however well-intentioned, can answer. It was Marian's mother who had been the instrument of the grace that healed, an aging woman of faith comforting her devastated daughter.

Rachel, our second grandchild, the first girl, has arrived, a little late, the day before my sixty-ninth birthday. She has thick dark hair like her father, like Mary Ellin, like my father and Mr. B. Half Eskimo papoose, half princess, she is all here.

WATER MILL

I AM READING Sean O'Faolain's last novel, written in his eighties, in which he celebrates the nastiness of old age: "Allow me to sing the quiet joys of age—all of them awaiting us as we approach the psalmist's three score and ten —debility, impotence, incontinence, diverticulitis, colonic cancer, stone in the gall bladder, sand in the eyes, a tongue like a henhouse, dullness of mind . . . friendless days, empty nights, muscular aches, markets falling, prices rising, pension contracting, no more plans, a slow rusting, coronaries, strokes . . ."

His answer to all these horrors is to send his hero backward through life—a nightmare solution if there ever was one—to enter success from the wrong end! Adolescence reversed! An inside out love affair! To be sure of every outcome!

If old age is worthless, a throwaway, or a dribble away, as O'Faolain would have us believe, what does that say to the rest of our life? The acknowledged value of old age sets the standard for everything between it and infancy—there is a searchlight in that last decade, whenever it comes, that illuminates everything before, and after as well, if we allow ourselves its full sweep.

I remember in the early 1950s my cousin Nellie hectoring Mr. B. about his attitude toward age—she was then past eighty, he barely sixty-five. With her own mother living to one hundred and two, and her grandmother—the famous D.A.R. Helen—living to one hundred, she saw her way clear to at least one hundred herself and she would have him do the same. Mary Ellin and I stood there on the sidelines observing these two with wonder, neither of whom looked within a decade of their age, or acted it for that matter. We watched them test each other in our apartment on Madison Avenue where they had both come to visit Elizabeth, the first Berlin grandchild. Neither of them won, nor for that matter lost.

So what does other people's old age have to do with my own old age and death? My parents, who died at sixty-eight and seventy-eight, never seemed old to me; no more did my mother-in-law in her eighties. Even Cousin Nellie, who at one hundred and three held the Barrett record for old age, still at one hundred, when I last saw her, seemed barely old—she was a little unsure of her facts perhaps, slipping generations. But she was still the Nellie who for decades had been the professional oldster, the Uncle Tom of old age, the unflagging Nellie who insisted upon posture, attitude— "don't slump, don't slouch, don't shuffle, head back, shoulders squared, demand a decent table, send back the bad wine, the inadequately cooked fish, the rancid butter"— who gave age no ground. She wore glasses, not because her eyesight was failing, but for cosmetic effect, her clothes were still carefully chosen, meticulously kept; there was no vagrant face powder on her bosom, no run-down heels or uneven hems.

Despite his protests to the contrary, Mr. B., always dapper, remained strangely unold through his eighties and into his nineties. I myself haven't seen him in a long time, nor am I likely to again. Even before his stroke he had become a disembodied voice on the telephone—no less, no more rasping than before, no quaver. Now there is a silence.

Mr. Dagmar seemed old because he wanted to, flaunted his age, acted the part with a will—old age was something he put on because he chose to—to get his way. If he wasn't a star in his prime, old age made him one, center stage, top of the bill in his one room flat, in his hospital bed.

All this makes old age seem indeterminate, vague—not at all definable in terms of afflictions, deficiencies, numbers.

You can peel it away. It is none of those things that O'Faolain says it is. Old age may sometimes be a weariness, or an absence of certain things perhaps, a loss by no means always detrimental, or to be regretted. It is the enhancement of others. It is vulnerabilities, but many invulnerabilities and the failures are of the body, the intellect, but not of the spirit, nor can they be. "Spirits" may sag or falter, but not the spirit. We are not in charge of that.

In recent months, maybe once or twice a fortnight, on the street, in a shop or restaurant, or the park I hear my name called. I turn and there is no one there, or no one to whom I can attribute the calling. I don't know whether I put together floating syllables or mistake someone else's name for my own. Perhaps it is an echo in my head of the bark of an earlier authority, or perhaps an authority yet to come. But the sound is clear and directed—"Marvin," out of thin air, or air thickened enough to extract those two distinct syllables.

SANTA MONICA

THE HOTEL EMBASSY, our Santa Monica headquarters, seems more my California than Mary Ellin's; it is the Southern California of my distant past. The cascading bougainvillea, a disconcerting magenta, hangs over one corner of the building, as old as the bricks beneath it. And the ornamental plantings, although neatly kept, seem just past their prime. Long past are the dark, dusty lobby with its heavily curtained French windows opening onto a sunless garden, the great black piano closed and locked, the dark Mission furniture, the library table covered with out-of-date magazines, the tiles thick with wax, the white-haired lady, bright-eyed in her cluttered cubicle.

It is the widow's and maiden lady's Southern California of my grandmother and spinster aunts, where a firm pudeur keeps the obscene sun at bay on behalf of the furnishings and rugs and pictures, lovingly packed, shipped all the way from Iowa in a not-so-hasty getaway. It is the tearoom and theosophical Southern California of fringed shawls and wispy hair escaping from elaborate buns, of carefully sheltered bank accounts, of Sundays in the park in the transplanted shade. This Southern California is not the brightly colored extravagant excess that Mary Ellin knew, the full sun of the Santa Monica beachfront, houses with big rooms, with big windows, each with its own swimming pool and sand and ocean for a front yard.

Still she likes our shabby room on the third floor with breakfast nook, kitchenette and a suitably 1930s Spanish style decor. The bathroom sink seems to be attached to the wall with chewing gum. No matter. It is clean and ours for a sixth of what a room in a fashionable hotel on Wilshire or Sunset would have cost us.

And into this, oblivious of such distinctions, bursts our two-year-old grandson, reactivating history. The pathos of that little blonde figure with his Dutch-boy haircut and his big visionary grey-blue eyes is overwhelming. His father releases him into our hotel room and he rushes across it and presents me with a small orange car, his favorite object of the moment.

On the other coast granddaughter Rachel at four months is still at the miraculous stage. Where did this wonderful little thing come from? What are her memories of that place she has deserted that give her that clear-eyed look? The squalling is irrelevant. It is the look.

Peter is beyond that look. Objects have taken over, and curiosity. He has gone from observation to discovery. He represents time spent—time to come—our pasts, his future —a sizable sweep.

The difference between love for one's children and one's grandchildren supposedly has to do with responsibility foresworn, enjoyment without the day-to-day care. It is obviously not that simple. It also has to do with posses- siveness, distance (not just of one coast from the other), and objectivity. One can see in those small creatures the real poignancy of childhood in a way one couldn't or did- n't with one's own when building the nest and gathering the worms seemed just as important as the chicks them- selves. But there was also the difference between a pang, and what else?—a panic. Am I doing it right? Is it Nature or nurture? Love forgotten for the moment in worry, in guilt. This after all is your choice, your fault: the fruit of your marriage bed. With grandchildren, a generation removed, there is little of that. Not panic—hope.

So you see little Peter coming across the hotel room toward you, clutching his beloved truck and then all of a sudden holding it out to you as an offering. Or Rachel look- ing up at you skeptically and then suddenly smiling. It is to swell your heart, if not break it. But the anxiety is gone.

"Becoming a grandfather," said Victor Hugo, "means stepping back into the dawn."

The first three days of our visit we woke to sun. Now we are having the long morning stretches of grey mist slowly burning off that I remember as the beginning of most California days, the bleakness that dissolves into a memory- obliterating dazzle. It is the darling of cliché makers—the cloud and its silver lining—the dark night and the dawn. At the heart of every cliché lies another more compelling and finally the truth.

"I do not seek to understand so that I may believe," said old St. Anselm. "But believe that I may understand. For this

I know to be true; that unless I first believe, I shall not understand."

To be born is to believe. To understand, watch Peter.

—⚹—

LAST NIGHT at Peggy and Sam Goldwyn's big house on a hill north of Sunset Boulevard—Mary Ellin's past revisited —I encountered my own past in a small, pretty, likable woman who said she was the novelist Judith Krantz. She suddenly revealed herself during dessert to be who she really was, Judy Tarcher, the best friend of Sue Kaufman, the girl I was in love with before Mary Ellin. Judy T., was last seen in New York in a large room overlooking Central Park, at a postwar party of bright young people, destinations unknown.

I sat there trying to bring it back—Judy, blonde as my friend Sue Kaufman was brunette, lively as Sue was languorous, the tingle of her nerves almost visible beneath her perfect surface. I was trying to bring back the picture without considering what had been lost and gained, who we were now and then, three young writers starting out in New York. I skirted the last tragic memories of Sue, her name made, her fear that she was unable to do it again. Meanwhile she fussed over her guests in her big upper East Side apartment that success, hers and her husband's, had bought her, her face, large-eyed, white-skinned, the mouth that as it smiled seemed always to want to weep; or in the Hamptons where she lay reflective beside her pool and raised a slender wrist to greet, to beckon us to her. The years never diminished the power she had over me, power expressed in one devastating final gesture of self-destruction. The power Judy was indicating right now was still in effect, a power that we sat there in silence, shaking our heads remembering. Tragedy's survivors.

So old age doesn't grant you the immunity you might have hoped for, not really. There are memories whose pain is proof of the seriousness of a life lived. Yours. Judy's. Sue's.

—⁓—

TODAY WAS GLORIOUS, clear and cool, following an unexpected rain. We took Elizabeth and Peter to the zoo where he seemed to have a particular affinity for its various forms of water—ponds, brooks, simulated rapids, and falls—and less for the animals, although wallowing in an appropriate puddle was a particularly splendid pink hippopotamus, shiny wet. After the zoo we went on to the train museum for a lunch of hot dogs and soda and a ride on the miniature railroad. Whenever I was taken on a major outing as a child (fairs, amusement parks) there always seemed to be a miniature railroad that looped through a make-believe landscape and brought you back to where you started, and if those in charge were sufficiently indulgent and the traffic wasn't too heavy, made a whole second circuit free of charge. Today, we, the three grownups and the one child, the only passengers, happily paid for our second turn, acknowledging that, right now, in California, everything has its price.

Mary Ellin went with me to see Uncle Bill, who brought out some snapshots, played one of her father's tunes on he pink piano, and told her how much that music had meant to him as a young man, and still did. "What'll I Do?"—he played it with a few skipped notes, an uncertain left hand. Mary Ellin left subdued by the memory of her parents, as they had once been in the Hollywood world of her youth. Her young mother, clever, fashionable, more so than any one else in the place and aware of it, was now gone. Her father, black hair and eyes, twice as alive, it seemed, as anyone else in the place, filled with songs, ideas for songs and shows, was now fading in his top floor bedroom, the angle of decline reported daily on the phone by her sister, the nurses. The memory of California as it once was—for her, for her parents—has nothing, nothing at all to do with old age.

NEW YORK

IT HAS FINALLY HAPPENED. Mr. B. died in his sleep the evening before last—at 5:30 P.M. The very fragile thread, but still a thread, was broken.

Mary Ellin had seen him on Thursday, reported to him on our trip—Peter, Elizabeth and Sasha, Sammy and Peggy—and told him that his old friend David Brown was bringing a show into the Music Box. He was sitting up, with his blind eyes open, barely responding—but he did respond, saying "Good," so faintly that she could scarcely hear. He was in better shape, the nurses said, than earlier in the week. However, Mary Ellin felt a difference that made her pause as she went through the doorway—as though there were something he had left unsaid—something she had left unasked and undeclared and there might not be another chance.

Friday morning we had driven to Cambridge, Massachusetts, to attend the dedication of the refurbished, expanded International Center given in memory of Minda de Gunzberg by her husband and sons. We arrived at the hotel at 3:30, went to the Signet clubhouse and had a Coke, bought Mary Ellin a raincoat and a housewarming present for Minda's younger son. We then returned to our hotel room. I drew a bath. The water came out pitch black. I called the front desk to see what could be done. The phone rang as I hung up. It was Alton to say that Mr. B. was dead.

These last few days have been filled and separated from any other reality. The endless tributes on TV, on radio, in the papers, none of which could we bring ourselves to listen to, watch, or read. The obituaries, the flowers, the condolences. The arrival of Mary Ellin's sister Linda and her husband Edouard from Paris, the arrangements for the funeral: no church, no synagogue, only the unannounced graveside service that Mr. B. had said he wanted, with thirty or so in attendance, mostly family and the old-timers from the office. The rabbi had been enlisted from Westchester where the cemetery was located. There were prayers and psalms, the Kaddish—no music, no eulogies.

Now there are the letters to be answered, the disposition of the effects—a process which promises to go on for months.

To die at one hundred and one—to hold off that long— simplifies none of these acts or the thoughts that come with them. Relief and regret still seem to strike the same balance and there are just that many more memories to be assimilated, leftovers to be disposed of.

And this death, if I permit myself to appropriate it to myself, is different from any other, binocular for me as the oldest of the next generation, the first son-in-law. I am the one who knew him when, whatever his protestations, he was still young and active, with a major hit, *Call Me Madam*, just opened on Broadway. Friendly and curious about his daughter's new beau, sharing his ideas for new movies and new Broadway shows. Visiting us in Taormina. Presiding over a family trip to Paris, Madrid, and Seville for Holy Week. He played host to the entire family, as it grew, at his retreat in the Catskills. Now I am sharing his death with those even closer to him than me, and also with millions of other people, headline readers, movie goers, TV viewers, record spinners, dancers, players, singers, who have a different reality of a man who slipped into my first memories, a quisling in that little bungalow on Forestdale Drive. His music was there on the player piano, its pre-punched paper rolls on the shelf next to the fireplace, the sheet music above the keyboard, with me since birth, with me along with an aging multitude on at least four of the seven continents. "The Song is Ended." I can still see its yellow cover, with a bridge, a melancholy cascade of flowers; the square ends of those piano roll boxes on the shelf under the Venetian glass vase: "Tell Me, Little Gypsy, What the Future Holds For Me," "Everybody Step." I remember the whispering click of the keys as I pumped the player piano pedals, my feet barely reaching them.

—∿—

IN MY SEVENTIETH YEAR I find myself suddenly rich, or if not rich myself (my pension actually was cut by a third six months ago), endowed by my parents-in-laws' deaths with a rich wife, well-off children, and all the trappings of wealth—a $20,000 wrist watch, a vicuna coat, two vicuna coats, the *Oxford English Dictionary*, all nine fat volumes, the complete Butler's *Lives of the Saints*, a library of fine bindings, our share of the family silver, china, furniture, paintings from three generations back, plus a set of cats eye cuff links, the kind I coveted when I was a shave-tail ensign in the New Hebrides, a handmade present from a noncom when he toured the South Pacific with *This Is the Army*.

Nor do I feel particularly burdened or corrupted by all these chattels. There has been too much else going on to distract me, too many others to concern myself with to have space to register corruption. And being in my seventieth year helps. The custodial aspect of possessions at such a time becomes very clear if one wants to acknowledge it. For how long will I be wearing those vicuna coats, that gold Cartier watch, poring over the OED and Butler, staring with smug possessiveness at all those fine bindings, eating off the blue and gold plates, flashing those cat's eye cufflinks?

"Woe to you who are rich, for you have received your consolation," St. Luke quotes the dampening words following his account of the Beatitudes. "Woe to you who are full now, for you will be hungry. Woe to you who are laughing now, for you will mourn and weep. Woe to you when all speak well of you, for that is what their ancestors did to the false prophets."

Old age effectively draws off most of the poison from those spoil-sport threats. What the Beatitudes state, old age simply reinforces. They are not choices, they are inevitabilities. To learn that lesson, you need only to survive. Meanwhile I am being instructed. The first day I wore my spectacular new coat, "like a movie star's or a race track tout's," the bum in front of Citibank told me admiringly, a few moments later a taxi splattered it with mud. My flashy watch gains ten minutes every twenty-four hours. The family china and silver are set on a high out-of-reach shelf. The fine books are yet, if ever, to be read. Neither the world nor the Lord seems to have gotten it quite right.

Furthermore, at my age, with my mortal diseases, I must be prepared to die at any moment. But then simply as a *mortal*, young or old, fit or failing, I say it yet again, I must be prepared for the same—by accident, by catastrophe, plague, war, the Four Horsemen, whatever.

This is a fact I have known since July 2nd, 1928 when Eddie, my responsibility, broke and ran and a second later, a split second later, was dead.

A harsh lesson—everyone's lesson—*the* lesson. So what is it?

Pay attention.
Pay attention then.
Pay attention now.

WATER MILL

IN LESS THAN A WEEK it will be Thanksgiving, then Christmas and New Year's. Tonight it is the nearly winter sky—Orion returned and all that goes with him. The sky is clear, moonless, with every star distinct. I walk Molly around the margin of the yard with the dark thickets and the corn field beyond and wonder what new arrangement of constellations, of holidays one will confront in the next stage of life, beyond death, out of this particular world. What will their replacements be in what we laughing uneasily call the hereafter? How will we cut through reality to reality? At what angle? What new disposition of hours and days will be revealed? There is no question that with all this temporal and spatial richness around us there will be a new frame, a new angle to view it all from, even if the reality is the same.

In the navy I used to see such skies. On board ship between Hawaii and San Francisco standing watch, a sky such as this arched above me, slid down into the deep surrounding purple and crept back up, with somewhere in that slow arc a slight hesitation as though the heavens were shifting gears. Before the watch was over I went to the railing and threw up.

So what watch is the proper analogy for old age?—naval watch or factory watch, that is (not the watch on my wrist or in my pocket). Is old age the swing watch from four to midnight or the mid watch from midnight to eight? I believe it is the latter, that long stretch before dawn and then the slide into light with its final release. I fear right now, right here, most of us think of old age as four to midnight, a going from a failing light into darkness, out into the surrounding dark.

There is misbehavior at the Thanksgiving table by me, and by Rachel, if a baby can really misbehave. Mine, as usual, has to do with words, twisting their meanings, making jokes where jokes aren't particularly welcome. Rachel's has to do with things, the misapplication of food. But are they that different in intent, in direction? The old can be, and frequently are, naughty in a way they haven't permitted themselves since childhood, and at least as frequently as children, they are allowed to get away with it. Indulged or ignored—one or the other. Naughtiness in the old and young is a potent weapon against the ages in between. Be naughty and let those who will be solemn or driven, virtuous or evil or whatever else the middle years require of them. But naughtiness is not the opposite of solemnity, or virtue or evil. It is of another nature and from another place.

Sometime between Thanksgiving and Christmas, at the IGA loading groceries into the back of the station wagon, my pants, insecurely fastened at the waist, fall to my ankles. Whatever the cause, a defective belt, loss of weight or muscle tone, inattention, I am at first startled, then with the perversity of infancy and old age, delighted. A burlesque turn there within full view of Montauk Highway. Question: Do the old have no shame? Answer: Not much.

Talking to myself: I began by talking to Molly who never replies and sometimes doesn't even respond with her soulful, vaguely troubled look. Then I began talking to pictures on the wall—Mary Ellin's elegant relatives and my parents: Poppa, two years old, in his English admiral's costume with a sword and a formidable lace blouse; Mother, the same age, bundled in furs. After that it was inanimate objects—milk pans that boil over, umbrellas that don't open. Now I have graduated to talking to myself—asking interesting questions, and giving answers, judgments, advice to the not yet present and the recently departed. It is all a great enrichment of life which comes, I suppose, from the blessed shamelessness of old age.

So the year has wound down, the year that found me suddenly inadvertently privileged as well as old. And what is privileged old age? We have some fairly clear pictures of privilege in younger life—of the infant with a silver spoon in its mouth, the poor little rich girl, the *jeunesse dorée,* the advantaged middle-aged with their luxuries, earned or inherited, swanking it.

But privileged old age is as difficult of definition and more certain of outcome than the privilege of infancy. Chauffeurs and lap robes, winters in a warm climate, the right masseuse, the right surgeon, the attention of a fashionable priest, an elegant clutter. Is that what our privilege consists in? If I thought so I wouldn't have brought it up.

Two citations for this year's holidays from *Christian Conversation,* Anne Fremantle's collection of "Catholic Thought for Every Day of the Year":

St. Honoratus of Arles, the fifth-century Gaul, to his students on his death bed:

You see how fragile is the house we inhabit. Whatever rank we hold, death comes upon us; neither riches nor honor can help us escape from his necessity. Live in such wise that you fear not the last hour, and look upon death as a journey. My dearly loved children, follow my advice, it is the only heritage your dying father and bishop can leave you. Do not allow yourselves to be deceived by love of the world. Relinquish voluntarily with your hearts that which you must one day involuntarily relinquish.

Or the example Brillat-Savarin gives in his *Physiology of Taste:*

> Death itself is not without charms when it is natural, that is to say, when a body has run the allotted course through the several phases of growth, maturing, old age, and decrepitude.
>
> I had a great aunt who lay dying at the age of ninety-three. Although she had for some time been confined to her bed, she was still in possession of her faculties, and her condition was perceived only through her gradual loss of appetite and failure of her voice.
>
> She had always shown great affection for me and I was at her bedside . . . "Are you there, nephew?" she said to me in scarcely articulate tones. "Yes, aunt, I am here to serve you and believe you would do well to drink a little good old wine." "Give it to me, my friend, liquid always goes downward." I quickly poured her half a glass of my best wine, and gently raising her, held it to her lips. She swallowed it and at once rallied; then turned on me her eyes which had once been very beautiful. "Many thanks," she said, "for this last service; if ever you should reach my age, you will find that death becomes a simple need, no less than sleep."

These were her last words, and half an hour later she had fallen asleep forever.

And finally Bill Sheed on his father Frank, famous for his street corner preaching:

> A man can be older at seventy than he is at eighty. Even before seventy Frank had begun to curse an imaginary loss of memory. He swore he could not recall half the songs that had formed his private background music for so long, or those ever-ready yards of Byron and Tennyson. He was an old man now, and he fully expected to act like one.
>
> By eighty, he was tired of all that: One can't sit around being old indefinitely. So the songs came back, and the zest to sing them.

In other words forget the inconveniences of old age, and enjoy it.

1990

1990___

THERE CAN BE PEACE PRECEDING DEATH according to tradition, even in the most agitated life. At least this peace is often reported by those present at the deaths not only of saints and people of undeniable virtue but also at those of warriors, firebrands, misanthropes, wastrels, the miserable, the tormented. It is my contention that this peace can be moved backwards into our lives, that the contemplation of our deaths can bring us a similar peace long before that final confrontation. Nor need this be a giving up, or an act of cowardice—quite the opposite, or not the opposite—a middle ground somewhere between cowardice and courage. Nor is it a grey, hopeless condition but instead a sort of exhilaration in place, a stationary joy neither going forward nor back—perhaps up, a levitation—a giving up in truth. But then joy never has had anything to do with before or behind or with future or past.

Last Saturday was Arthur Gold's memorial in Oak Lawn Cemetery in Sag Harbor. We had seen Arthur, seventy-two, in his Manhattan apartment a fortnight or so ago, in no way diminished by the illness which was shortly to kill him. Lying in bed, the covers up to his armpits, his hands and elbows free, there was no sense of wasting. His face was as cheerful and bright as always, as was his spirit. He had chosen not to have radical chemotherapy which would have prolonged his life, and when he was taken to the hospital during a crisis, he elected to return to the apartment and die there. His doctor, Jerry Barondess, told Bobby Fizdale, his partner and companion of fifty years, that his was the most dignified death he had ever witnessed; and Arthur, to the best of my knowledge, had no compensatory belief in anything to explain that dignity.

He was buried not too far from his good friends, Carmen Namuth and George Balanchine. A large group congregated to listen to the eulogies, well meant and inadequate as such tributes usually are, and then to line up and tell Bobby how sad we all were. Inadequate too.

In an article on Archbishop Romero in *Commonweal,* Monsignor Urioste says, "Death is a theological not a biological event."

—⚹—

YESTERDAY I WENT TO SEE WILLY KNAPP, my college roommate and oldest friend, who sits in his chair in his back parlor in Westport, Connecticut surrounded by pillows. We talked and he dozed off and then we talked again. Although he was lucid when awake, he was childish and notional about food, the disposition of pillows, etc. There has been a failure in his energies for a year or two, a hastening of the aging process partially due I am sure to physical failure —(he had a valve replacement in his heart—a pig's valve, he liked to point out; seven hours on the operating table) and partly perhaps by choice.

He showed a deliberate indecision on stairs, about which pill to take, about forks—though not about words, never about words—which amounted to a declaration of mortality, a decline in energy and now a drastic immobilization.

What is Willy's view of death? I wouldn't consider asking him although I remember his describing, as though it had a special significance for him and for me as well, a visit with a colleague to the room where Delmore Schwartz, one of the few acknowledged geniuses of our youth, had just died alone surrounded by dust, grime, and dozens of disheveled girlie magazines. There is little out of place in the Knapp's back parlor, or anywhere in their tall Victorian farmhouse, nor indeed has there ever been in Willy's orderly and friendly life. Peggy, his wife, who remains sprightly though herself ailing in various conspicuous ways, reported that every time she runs into Peter deVries in the supermarket he exclaims, "Remnants! Nothing but remnants!" or "Bits and pieces, bits and pieces!" She looks at me as though she agrees.

Neither description applied to Arthur, nor to Willy, frail though he was, but still all of a piece, nor certainly to Canon West, aged eighty, who could freeze with a glance a frivolous twenty-year-old. The Canon lived in an apartment on the top floor of Diocesan House surrounded by a confusion of books, pious objects, Golden Retrievers, and concerned and obliging young men. I attended his funeral at the Cathedral this morning, a twenty-minute procession, maybe two hundred clergy and others participating. Two and a half hours in all, a triumph of sorts for one dead clergyman, keeping us all there in that salutary environment, motionless and thoughtful, for that long.

"Throughout my life, through my life, the world has little by little caught fire in my sight until, aflame all around me, it has become almost completely luminous from within . . . such has been my experience in contact with the earth—the diaphany of the divine at the heart of the universe on fire . . ." So wrote Teilhard de Chardin at the end of life when he was surrounded by disbelief and scorn.

Willy, a stubborn non-believer like most of my generation, is resisting any such revelation. Arthur lay there as if saying *I am waiting to see.* Canon West, leaving the clutter behind him, moved right on in.

—⚭—

THREE MONTHS PAST her youngest child's death of AIDS, Barbara E. and I remembered her son at lunch today. Sean was an intelligent, good-looking boy in his late twenties whom the whole family—his parents, his sister, his twin brothers, and his ninety-year-old Irish grandmother— united to support and attend in his futile two-year struggle against death. His going seems the antithesis of Arthur's or Willy's or Canon West's, a young man's dogged fight for every inch of relinquished mortality. There are pictures of him in his wheelchair at his sister's wedding, days before his death—an old, wasted young man with a dark shadow on one cheek and eyes straight on, blind, behind glasses— sitting there surrounded by his family, erect, square-shouldered in their wedding clothes.

The last time I saw Sean he was waiting table for Glorious Foods at a big cathedral party in Synod House, still whole and handsome, no sign of his disease upon him, although by then he had already gone through several desperate episodes, chills so violent that a dozen blankets were useless, his brothers and parents taking turns lying beside him to warm him. But when I saw him, he was performing heroic feats, running up a dozen flights at Memorial Hospital, to prove that the treatment which everyone except his family suspected was useless, was indeed working.

As you grow older your hope in miracles, in luck, in happy accidents, immunity, disappears along with your dread of the opposite. The miracle is not something that happens to you—it is all around you, you are embedded in it, moving through it, part of it. For the old, disaster and suffering are one more means of realizing and acting out the second great commandment, binding your neighbor to yourself. But that conviction is not for the young, nor the grieving, nor anyone indeed but oneself. I, beyond death, can affirm the all-encompassing miracle that Arthur, Canon West, Sean, and now Willy are moving through.

I began this particular passage of my life in death. It will end in the same place and that place I already have experienced as bright and green, green as in growing, bright as in knowing.

—ɯ—

MR. B.'S MEMORIAL SERVICE. People were lined up at six in the morning on 45th Street outside the Music Box, the kind of crowd Mr. B. would have appreciated. Standing room only, people cadging seats, dozens turned away.

Kitty Hart was up there again, in a blue dress this time, as vibrant as the red she wore for his hundredth birthday.

The memorial was a celebration with a long list of old friends and admirers sharing their memories and playing and singing his songs. However fine the reminiscences, it was the songs that counted. Just reciting the songs' names would have been enough. The words and music were in our heads.

Back in the library at Beekman Place which has been put up for sale, we were told that one of the Maguire Sisters out in Las Vegas had offered seven million if we'd throw in one of Mr. B.'s pianos.

ITALY

HOTEL PALUMBO, RAVELLO. We are here on a fortnight holiday before Mary Ellin begins research on the memoir of her father that she has committed herself to write. She has abandoned her novel to take on something far more difficult, her own life and her family's. That means, once we have caught our breath, visits to Caserta, Santa Maria da Capua, to the north, and Foggia and Bari in the south, ending in Naples and Rome, places where her father took *This Is the Army* during the war. Already Mary Ellin has begun to fill a college-size notebook.

Our hotel room is square, white, simply furnished for a place which boasts of being the second most expensive accommodation on the Amalfi coast. There is a barrel vault overhead and a solarium terrace set facing the view.

Now at eight A.M. it is amazingly quiet for Italy—no traffic, no animal or human noise. I look out over a garden with lemon trees covered with protective black plastic and a large naked grape arbor. Beyond is the rugged coastline and the Gulf of Salerno, silver this morning and smooth under clouds. The same outlook, of mountains and sea, as from Casa Talio in Taormina, from the promenade in Santa Monica looking north. Coast, sky, and in the distance mountains. The garden is deserted. Mary Ellin's notebook is open on the bedside table.

Yesterday we went to Paestum, down the hill from Ravello and along the shore into the view, retracing the first stretch of our honeymoon, when we were on our own, the two of us, heading into unknown territory in our Hillman Minx. We had arrived at a farm inn after dark, eaten a late dinner of cold and gummy pasta in the farm kitchen; our room was bare with a lumpy bed and the sound of rats in the walls. The next morning the soap, our own, had been gnawed half away. The innkeepers, already paid, were out of sight. We dressed, shivering, and went into the yard. There they were—the ancient grey-black temples—in a grey-black drizzle. As we approached for a closer look a flock of rooks flapped out of the eaves and away into the wet grey sky.

Thirty-seven years later, our experience was something quite different, proof that things don't inevitably go to pot. The temples in a bright green meadow were bordered by flowering trees, dazzling, and rookless; we saw three temples now instead of two (could we have missed a temple before?), cleaner and more substantial even than the golden ones of Sicily—plus an amphitheater, a forum, stone streets, the foundations of houses in an ordered litter that was certainly out of sight on our earlier visit. We wandered and sat and stared and then went to have lunch in the old farm house, now a pricey restaurant with state-of-the-art plumbing. The Paestum of youth and old age, now side by side in memory.

In the little museum there was a painted tomb cover with a young athlete blithely diving into some undefined puddle. On a wall at Herculaneum or Pompeii such a painting would be symbol for the beginning of a carefree privileged life; on a tomb at Paestum it is death the young man is diving into with the same abandon.

Across the Gulf of Salerno under a daytime moon and open sky are two white boats with separate destinations heading toward each other.

After our circuit of Campania and Apulia we are in Naples to rendezvous with the Steegmullers. Shirley, pretty as always, talkative—when she talks you listen—is working on her next novel. Francis, aged eighty-six, is preparing two major works of scholarship for publication next year. Francis with serene urbanity acknowledges nothing remarkable in these demanding undertakings at his age, at any age. One does what one can do, must do, and keeps on doing it. His cane is a recent compromise.

. . .

Rome. We make a hasty visit to the Chiesa Nuova, the church of San Filippo Neri, one of my favorite holy men (haven't I named Pippo my cat after him?), whom a sixteenth-century contemporary described as "A beautiful old man, clean and white, like an ermine, his flesh is delicate and virginal and if, when he lifts his hand, he holds it up to the sun, it is transparent like alabaster." Like Gerald's hand held against the California sun, like Father Griffiths' against the hottest sun of all.

Nothing in the dark interior of the church evokes the light-hearted, transparent spirit of the father of the Oratory Order who spent his last years entertaining and encouraging the young. No one sits in the shadows but us and a middle-aged man bent forward, half on his knees, with a ravaged, semi-mad face. Eventually a young verger in a white shirt and black pants comes in, impatient for us to leave so he can close and lock the place.

The final paragraph of Jung's memoirs, deposited now on the bedside table at our Rome hotel:

> When Lao-tsu says, "All are clear, I alone am clouded," he is expressing what I now feel in advanced old age. Lao-tsu is the example of a man with superior insight who has seen and experienced worth and worthlessness, and who at the end of his life desires to return into his own being, into the eternal unknowable meaning. The archetype of the old man who has seen enough is eternally true. At every level of intelligence this type appears, and its lineaments are always the same, whether it be an old peasant or a great philosopher like Lao-tsu. This is old age and a limitation. Yet there is so much that fills me: plants, animals, clouds, day and night and the eternal in man. The more uncertain I have felt about myself, the more has grown up

in me a feeling of kinship with all things. In fact it seems to me as if that alienation which so long separated me from the world has become transferred into my own inner world and has revealed to me an unexpected unfamiliarity with myself.

Jung, old, as if in Buchenwald. We old create our own Buchenwald and turn it to our own uses.

NEW YORK

WE ARE SETTLING BACK INTO CITY LIFE after our month in Italy. That sense of precariousness, of not knowing what comes next which is strangely absent when we are away from home, has returned. This precariousness I would say is more frequent in old age than earlier and, at any time in life, means that you are about to learn something.

Yesterday we made up the invitation list for my seventieth birthday party, a self-consciously important event to be held in a hall which I am told is at the top of Radio City and can accommodate at least one hundred.

Last night in wakeful stretches, instead of my usual series of intercessions, I found myself seating or trying to seat the luncheon—the names of the about-to-be-invited replacing the names of the loved and the needful—although many of them are the same.

The old man with the cane—perhaps five years my senior—whom I see every day walking slowly up 116th Street and on down Broadway with no discernible destination, seems, at least to me, to be performing a sacrament. His pace has been slowed so that it conforms not to the busy, hurried young and middle-aged people of a university community bustling about him, but to another deeper, internal clock.

All activity, neutral or benign, I believe can be made to conform to that clock: domestic chores, eating, preparing food, caring for an animal, weeding a garden, walking up a hill without a destination. That is what observant Jews and Hindus acknowledge early on; for the rest of us this realization tends to come much later, with the natural slowing down of our functions. The failing of our memory may help. Why am I in the kitchen? What was the errand to the back of the apartment that I forgot by the time I reached the bedroom door? Why does that person coming toward me look so familiar? Why is he smiling as though he knows me, raising his hand in greeting? The whole world looks familiar.

A dream of Greta Garbo, who died last week, in her long bulky coat and deep brimmed hat. She nods. I nod. "You have been married nine times," she says to me accusingly. Then she turns to Mary Ellin who is walking beside me. "He always says 'hello,' but you never do." "Mary Ellin is short-sighted besides being my only wife," I explain. Then I realize she is being complimentary, that it is Mary Ellin's infinite variety that she is referring to. The dream fades and she is gone. And now gone in truth. Only the memory remains, vivid, of the unforgettable film *Camille* and Garbo its star, sitting in the row ahead of us, as on stage Maria Callas, La Traviata, sings her heart out. A double and not quite congruent vision.

Recently my dreams have not been so entertaining but instead are rather depressed and grim. Bleak dreams I guess are the price I pay for waking serenity. The bleaker the dream, the brighter the morning I wake into.

. . .

Going downtown to dinner with friends the taxi driver annoys me by ignoring my advice to head south through the park. Instead he crosses at 86th and turns right onto Fifth Avenue. And there suddenly in front of us, after an afternoon of heavy rain, the buildings have turned white gold, whiter and more golden even than the towers of New Jersey I used to see as they caught the rising sun on my morning walks through Riverside Park. A blazing illumination, an incomparable dazzle, shimmering there on the quivering edge of being understood, like the revelations of dying adolescence or old age just beginning. And then we proceed down Fifth arriving at our destination ten minutes early.

At eighteen it is natural for everything to seem bright and filled with possibility. At nearly seventy the possibilities are either realized (unlikely) or, one hopes, forgotten. And there suddenly in front of you, with you going toward it, is the bright wall of Central Park South, promising once more everything. Like Blair at morning service saying the only AIDS patients he knows, and he knows many, who are happy and serene are the ones who have accepted the imminence of their death.

"So that with much ado I was corrupted, and made to learn the dirty devices of the world," says Thomas Traherne, "which now I unlearn, and become, as it were, a little child again that I may enter into the kingdom of God."

The trick is not only the unlearning, but making it last.

Today, walking up the 116th Street hill to Broadway, the same hill and walk the old man with the cane takes daily, I feel myself caught in some sort of interior pantomime, a succession of brief tableaux. Baby Marvin—I have found a picture of me, really me this time—a bald, round-headed two-month-old looking out at the world, half perplexed, half amazed. Next it is Marvin, age three, blonde bowl hair-cut, in powder blue soakers and jersey opening my mouth for some Dutch sweetmeat Aunt Elizabeth has made me. Then it's Marvin at twelve, an attendant in the Callanan Junior High May Queen's court, wearing short black pants, white wide-sleeved blouse run up on Mother's sewing machine, a loose beret pulled over one eye—the most popular boy on the West End of Des Moines with one possible exception. Next, Marvin at the bus station outfitted for Harvard in electric blue trousers, crew neck sweater, crew cut, sneakers. Not for long. Marvin the provisional ensign in a Brooks Brothers uniform with a Brooks Brothers double-calf suitcase heading west. Marvin in a beard, delving and praying, Marvin pushing a pram, pulling a child out of the surf, bringing a son or daughter home from school, from college. Marvin young or middle-aged on a stage, with the house lights up, the whole world, presumably, watching. All these Marvins are climbing slowly up the hill with me, pretending to be a man of seventy. It is not the first time I have caught myself out like this—young playing old, clever playing dim, hale playing ailing. A dreaming butterfly flapping about the city.

At the market, surrounded by every stage and condition of life save my own, during the late morning rush hour, they see me for what, for who I am—a man now twenty years older than the first time he came past this check-out counter and looking every minute of it.

At some point certainly you should stop writing about old age—thinking about it—fussing about it—and simply do it. I haven't reached that point yet, and possibly never shall. Still, it is worth heading toward.

—〽—

I AM SEVENTY. In the apartment on Claremont Avenue Petey Matson is creating his own marvelous three-year-old world on our living room carpet. A folding rule becomes a vacuum cleaner; there are tinker toy hammers, pumps, ladders, tools for building a world with no boundaries. For me, at the other end, the barricades are going down as well, so that before I slip off the edge I can, if I wish, have a view as unobstructed as the one I had yesterday, out into a peerless May day, sixty-five stories up.

At the celebration in the Rainbow Pavillion at the top of Radio City, seventy years old for sure, nearly everyone who was anyone in my life and had survived was in attendance, starting with Mary Ellin who mounted the whole thing, our four children, our three sons-in-law, our two grandchildren, my brother, my nephew, two nieces, two sisters-in-law, a couple of ex-bosses, ninety-four guests, all told.

And there it was—the narrow vibrating green of Central Park, its unchanged, unchanging rectangle pointing as a finger out from the narrow bar-lounge crowded with happy talk, to the bridges and on, pointing seemingly forever, into Westchester and whatever lay beyond—Connecticut, Harvard, the rockbound coast of Maine where we all spent a summer the year I lost my job and Mary Ellin was working on her first novel.

To the south through the high windows of the dining room were the topless towers of Manhattan and past them the bay into which all those boats bearing fathers, grandfathers, great-grandfathers, forefathers and foremothers sailed.

To the east was Long Island all the way to Water Mill and on to Spain, Italy, the Holy Land, India.

Even New Jersey seemed a miracle. Especially a miracle which, should we stand on our tippy toes, would draw apart to reveal Chicago, Des Moines, California, the South Pacific, all our pasts.

Indeed it was a miracle in every direction with us for that celebratory moment at its center.

And so, maybe for the first time, situated thus at the very apex of privilege, surrounded by those I love, a clear view in all directions, looking out with seriousness, steadiness, expectant attention, I can ask myself with conviction as any one who admits to seventy should: "Who am I? Why am I here? Where am I heading? Who, after all ('after all' being the operative phrase), am I?"

Soon enough, expectation will become likelihood and likelihood, certainty. And then . . . as Rumi observed in a land I have never, nor am likely ever to visit:

> *If death be a man let him come close to me*
> *That I may clasp him firmly to my breast!*
> *I'll take from him a soul, pure, without color;*
> *He'll take from me a colored frock, no more!*

But not quite yet.

Afterword

NOT QUITE YET has now stretched into eight eventful years. I have tried several times to write a proper epilogue but it always comes out sounding like a long-winded, overly sprightly alumni note for Harvard class of '42.

To be brief, I have seen the arrival of three splendid new grandsons—Benjamin Lerner, James Matson, and Nicholas Swett—and an equally splendid daughter-in-law, Julie Guttrich Barrett. Peter Matson is now a stalwart eleven; Rachel Swett, a winsome and resourceful nine.

Having been given so rewarding an additional eight years I may look forward to the future more than I should. There is a book to sell and another to complete, the millennium to usher in, my eightieth birthday to celebrate, our fiftieth anniversary, the high school graduation of Peter and Rachel and all the rest. There will always be an opportunity to learn, and to pray, and less and less to dread.

So this final note is, God willing, *au revoir,* but not goodbye.

Index

PARABOLA Books are published by *The Society for the Study of Myth and Tradition*, a not-for-profit, non-denominational educational organization. The *Society*'s goal is to produce and distribute literary, cultural, and educational works which illuminate the human search for meaning as it is expressed through the myths, symbols, rituals and sacred disciplines of the world.

Other books you may enjoy include:

Elders on Love: Dialogues on the Consciousness, Cultivation, and Expression of Love, by Kenneth Lakritz, Ph.D. and Thomas Knoblauch, Ph.D ($15.95)

Old Age: Journey into Simplicity, by Helen M. Luke ($9.95)

The Parabola Book of Healing, edited by Lawrence E. Sullivan ($22.95)

And There Was Light: The Autobiography of Jacques Lusseyran, Blind Hero of the French Resistance, translated by Elizabeth Cameron ($14.95)

Living by Wonder: The Imaginative Life of Childhood, by Richard Lewis ($18.95)

I Become Part of It: Sacred Dimensions in Native American Life, edited by D.M. Dooling and P. Jordan-Smith ($14.95)

Since 1976, the *Society* has also published the award-winning journal, PARABOLA Magazine. Marvin Barrett is a Senior Editor of PARABOLA and a frequent contributor of articles to the journal.

PARABOLA: *Myth, Tradition, and the Search for Meaning* (One year subscription, 4 issues, $24.00)

For a complete catalog of PARABOLA publications, please call or write to: PARABOLA, 656 Broadway, New York, N.Y. 10012. (212) 505-6200 ❖ (800) 560-MYTH ❖ www.parabola.org